BOUGHTON

The House, its People and its Collections

*'We saw Boughton, the noble seat of the Duke of Mountague, a house built at the cost and by the fancy
of the late Duke, very much after the model of the Palace of Versailles…
the house itself is very large and magnificent, but the situation facing so beautiful a park adds to
the glory of it: the park is wall'd round with brick, and so finely planted with trees,
and in such an excellent order, as I saw nothing more beautiful, no not in Italy itself,
except that the walks of trees were not orange and limon, and citron, as it is in Naples,
and the Abruzzo, and other southern parts of Italy.'*

Daniel Defoe 'A Tour Through the Whole Island of Great Britain, 1724–26'

Richard, Duke of Buccleuch and Queensberry

Edited by John Montagu Douglas Scott

Photographs by Fritz von der Schulenburg

Preface

It is 45 years since the distinguished architectural writer John Cornforth coined the phrase 'The English Versailles' in a series of articles about Boughton for *Country Life* magazine. It found immediate resonance, as much among my family as among fellow country-house historians, as a neat encapsulation of this extraordinary complex of buildings.

To understand the point, one need look no further than the great North Front, its formidable façade topped by mansard roofs and set low in a roll of gentle parkland. Come inside and the evidence of French artistry and craftsmanship, predominantly that of Huguenot refugees fleeing persecution by Louis XIV, abounds not just in great painting and fine furniture but in the necessities of life – window glass, mirrors, candlesticks. All find a companionable home alongside their contemporary English equivalents.

If anything the soubriquet seems even more deserved now, since the intervening years have witnessed the removal of centuries of vegetative overlay that had concealed huge formal gardens, with canals and lakes and parterres, the work in the French style of Leonard van der Meulen.

Yet as time passes the complexity of Boughton keeps resurfacing and the puzzles of its identity and purpose grow again. I rather suspect it has been a puzzle for generations of my family, not certain whether or when or how to use it. As a straightforward Tudor manor of the 16th and 17th centuries, it would no doubt have been logical and functional for the Montagus, a family of relatively unambitious lawyers and country gentlemen making their way slowly up the titled pecking order. It was like a self-sufficient village, with bakery, brewery, laundry and stables, at the heart of the agricultural estate on which their wealth was founded, gradually evolving with necessity and invention.

When, however, at the end of the 17th century my ancestor Ralph, carried away by his experiences on the Continent and flush with the fortunes of two successive brides, dropped a slice of France into Northamptonshire, it was, one feels, about dreams and vanity more than practicality. In his lifetime the house appears to have worked as a place of occasional and magnificent bursts of entertaining, even if the prized visit by the King happened but once, in 1695. The French émigré Charles de Saint-Évremond laments his inability in later life to join the glorious throng: 'I never desired anything so earnestly as to go to Boughton to see my Lord, the good Company and Learning in its full lustre.'

For Ralph's son John, a kind and modest man of inquiring mind, Boughton seems again to have provided a welcome escape from London, but was enjoyed rather differently. He loved nothing better than to ride the miles of avenues he had planted, particularly those that led to his favourite daughter and her husband up the road at Deene Hall. Elsewhere, even he appears to have recognised the impracticality of some of his father's building ambitions. He retreated from the palatial Montagu House in London, which was to become the home of the British Museum not long after his death, for something altogether more practical, cosy even, beside the Thames. It was a pattern that was to be repeated.

Mary, his daughter and heir, and her husband, George, made little use of Boughton, and their daughter Elizabeth and her husband, Henry, 3rd Duke of Buccleuch, a many-propertied Scottish landowner, even less. And so it continued until relatively recently.

My family has generally explained this neglect on the grounds that they were spoilt for choice, with too many houses and not enough time in the year, and of course that was true. But I think it was compounded by a sense of Boughton's impracticality. The creature comforts of warm food and hot running water, increasingly taken for granted in the Victorian era, came to be missed.

Indeed the struggle against the winter cold – guests are warned to put their coats on to come into the house – accounts for the fact that, even when my grandparents and parents did come to love it again, they came here only from May to July. But then they brought it vividly to life with the chatter and laughter of visiting friends and house parties. It became once more something of a stage set...

Richard, Duke of Buccleuch and Queensberry

OPPOSITE JOHN BAPTIST CLOSTERMAN, C. 1700
Ralph, 1st Duke of Montagu (1638–1709)

Contents

Left The park at Boughton, with its long vistas and 17th-century canals. Plans for an elaborate Gothic-style bridge over the River Ise in the distance were fortunately abandoned

The dawn of a dynasty

The early story of the Montagus of Boughton begins at the court of Edward I and Eleanor of Castile and ends with the unfortunate Ned, who rashly squeezed Catherine of Braganza's hand

For anyone with an interest in heraldry, the family history of the Montagus is writ large and repeatedly in coats of arms and family trees scattered around Boughton, above fireplaces in monochrome stone or painted plaster or carved woodwork, in escutcheon friezes along the walls and down the treads of a staircase. Dukes Ralph and John were fascinated by, and proud of, their descent. They believed that Drogo de Monte Acuto had brought the name over with William the Conqueror, and they were convinced that a later marriage link gave them descent from the highest in the land, King Edward I and his Queen, Eleanor of Castile. By happy coincidence the unfortunate consort, who died in 1290 at Harby, near Lincoln, was even commemorated within the

LEFT JEREMIAH VAN DER EYDEN (D.1695)
Ralph de Monthermer, 1st Baron Monthermer, Earl of Gloucester, Hertford and Atholl (c.1270–325)
The Montagus' illustrious ancestor, as imagined by the artist. Monthermer married the daughter of Edward I and Eleanor of Castile. Four centuries later, the name was used as the courtesy title of the eldest son
RIGHT *Coats of arms on the heraldic fireplace in the Little Hall. The lozenges were Montagu, the eagles Monthermer. The 1st Lord Montagu was challenged in court for bearing the eagles in 1605*

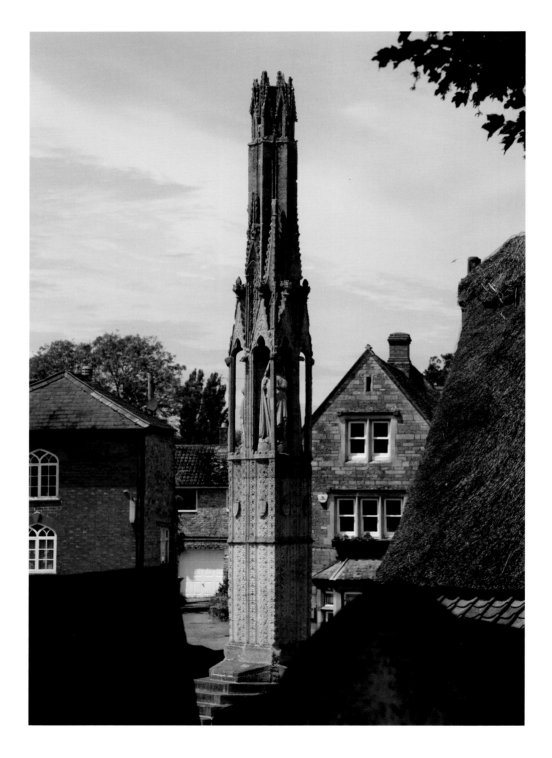

estate boundaries. The tall and beautiful Eleanor Cross that stands at the heart of nearby Geddington village was erected by her grieving husband to mark the spot where her casket rested on its journey for burial in Westminster Abbey.

To reinforce their conviction, the Dukes had portraits painted of their legendary ancestors. The earliest is supposedly Ralph de Monthermer, Earl of Gloucester, Hertford and Atholl, who lived between about 1270 and 1325 and married Joan of Acre, the daughter of King Edward and Queen Eleanor. It was therefore very posthumously that he was portrayed c.1690 by Jeremiah van der Eyden as a knight in shining armour.

Without wanting to cast too much doubt on this version of our descent, which depends on two cloudy links through the female line, it can be said with confidence that there were Montagus residing in Northamptonshire from the 15th century. One Richard Ladde adopted his mother's name of Montagu around 1448 and held property at Hanging Houghton in the centre of the county. Thomas, his son, and his wife, Agnes, were the parents of the early hero of the Montagu story, Edward, later Sir Edward. They have a fine memorial brass in Hemington Church, in the east of the county, where they lived in the manor.

LEFT THE ELEANOR CROSS, 1292
This beautiful triangular monument at Geddington bordering the park at Boughton is a miraculous survivor after more than seven centuries. Near the site of a royal hunting lodge, it marks one of the 12 resting places of the cortège bearing the body and heart of Edward I's beloved Queen, Eleanor of Castile, to London in 1290. The Montagus claimed descent from the royal couple via their daughter. Restored by the 2nd Duke of Montagu in 1745, this is the best-preserved of the three original crosses still standing

The 1st Sir Edward Montagu (c.1490–1557)

Born in the early years of Henry VII's reign, the 1st Sir Edward Montagu had a successful career as a lawyer, which enabled him to buy one of the two manors at Boughton in 1528, then several nearby manors – Weekley, Warkton, Geddington, and Barnwell to the east – before he finally purchased the second of the Boughton manors from St Edmundsbury's Abbey in Suffolk in 1536.

Henry VIII's Dissolution of the Monasteries provided rich opportunities for those in royal favour. Edward Montagu, a shrewd lawyer who worked for the Abbot of Peterborough, attracted the King's attention in a curious way as early as 1524, when he was given permission to 'use and wear his bonnet' in the royal presence, because of unspecified 'infirmities' troubling his head. He was knighted in 1537 and became Chief Justice of the King's Bench in 1539. In 1545 he was made Chief Justice of the Common Pleas and was one of the Commissioners of King Henry's will.

Rather less propitiously, he was also involved in the drafting of Edward VI's will, which named Lady Jane Grey as successor rather than Princess Mary. This led to a perilous period of imprisonment in the Tower of London, and Sir Edward was saved only by his written testimony of contrition, the draft of which survives in the archives at Boughton, and by a substantial sum of money. He died in 1557 and is buried with his wife Cecily in nearby Weekley church.

Sᵗ. Edward Mountagu off Boughton knight .
Cheeff Justice off bothe Benches .
Priue Counceler vnto Two Kinges
On off the Executers to King. H. 8.
obyt Anno Dom . 1 5 5 6 .

Above **English School**
The 1st Sir Edward Montagu
(1490–1557)
In this portrait in the Great Hall, Sir Edward wears the gold chain of Chief Justice of the Common Pleas. He used the three lozenges for the first time to seal his purchase of Boughton in 1536
Left *His effigy at St Mary the Virgin, Weekley*

The 2nd Sir Edward Montagu (1531–1602)

The 1st Sir Edward was succeeded by his son and namesake. An almost exact contemporary of Elizabeth I, the 2nd Sir Edward seems not to have had ambitions to advance himself at court or in the law, being content instead to reap the rewards of a wealthy country landowner. He had his merchant brother, Roger, buy him luxuries in London such as fine Gascon wine, clothes, spices and apricot trees.

He played the part of a county administrator when necessary and was knighted in 1568. In 1587 he was present at the execution of Mary, Queen of Scots at Fotheringhay Castle, near Peterborough. One of his higher-profile tasks was raising county men to defend the country against the Spanish Armada in 1588. Sir Edward's troops were late for the muster, and Sir Richard Knightley, who had raised the other half of the county, was rather irritated to have to wait at St Albans.

Sir Edward and his wife, Elizabeth Harington, were best remembered for their six remarkable sons. The eldest, Edward, became Lord Montagu in 1621. Sir Charles Montagu of Barking was a gallant soldier who saved 500 lives in Ireland and resigned

his commission rather than pander to Queen Elizabeth 'like a dog at the door'. James was the first Master of Sidney Sussex College, Cambridge, then later Bishop of Bath and Wells. He restored Bath Abbey and revived the legend of the Glastonbury Thorn.

Sir Sidney Montagu of Hinchingbrooke was a judge whose son Edward was one of the most influential figures of his day, being created Earl of Sandwich in 1660. Henry, the youngest son, was also a judge and leading politician in the run-up to the Civil War. His descendants became Dukes of Manchester. When James I feasted at Boughton in 1604, two years after the 2nd Sir Edward's death, each course was presented by one of the six Montagu brothers.

OPPOSITE ENGLISH SCHOOL, 1591
The 2nd Sir Edward Montagu (1531–1602)
Painted at 60, the silver-bearded 2nd Sir Edward's dour appearance conceals a more relaxed character
OPPOSITE, LEFT *His effigy in the parish church of St Mary the Virgin, Weekley*
LEFT CIRCLE OF CORNELIUS JANSEN
Elizabeth Harington, Lady Montagu (1545–1618)
A moving portrait of the 2nd Sir Edward's wife, and mother of his six remarkable sons, painted when blind in widow's weeds
BELOW *The overmantel in the Flower Gallery (page 154) came from the Montagu manor at Barnwell and shows the 2nd Sir Edward's family descent. His son Edward added the arms of his first two wives either side of the fireplace after 1612*

'Honest and faithful', the 1st Lord Montagu (1562–1644)

Like all his Montagu brothers, the 3rd Sir Edward, who eventually became the 1st Lord Montagu, was a strong supporter of the reformed Protestant religion. But James I of England and VI of Scotland, the son of Mary, Queen of Scots, was suspicious of extremes, and in 1605 Sir Edward managed to arouse his ire by supporting a petition on behalf of dispossessed Puritan ministers. The King regarded such petitions as 'little less than treason', and Sir Edward had to write a letter explaining himself, which his brother James, then Dean of the Chapel Royal, took to the

ABOVE ADRIAEN HANNEMAN
The 1st Lord Montagu of Boughton (1562–1644)
The 3rd Sir Edward became Lord Montagu in 1621 and was the subject of both contemporary and modern biographies. He died at the ripe old age of 88, at the height of the Civil War, under house arrest by the Parliamentary side suspicious of his loyalty to the King. Hanneman's portrait hangs in the Great Hall, where there were daily

morning and evening prayers and two psalms were sung after supper. James I considered he 'smelt a little of Puritanism'
LEFT *Standing sculptures of the 1st Lord Montagu and his first wife, Elizabeth Jeffrey, can be seen in the parish church of Chiddingly, near Eastbourne, her family home, either side of her father's reclining effigy. Their daughter kneels in the foreground*

King. James I was not entirely convinced, and it is in this context that Sir Edward's reaction to the Gunpowder Plot should perhaps be seen. The plot implicated the Treshams and other Northamptonshire landowners. Sir Edward, keen to prove his absolute loyalty to the King, took the lead in tabling the Act of Parliament whereby November 5 was turned into an official day of thanksgiving.

The King relied on men such as Montagu to maintain the peace in the counties. One of the most serious instances of civil unrest was the Midland Revolt in the spring and early summer of 1607, when there were protests and riots over the enclosure of open farmland. These came to a head on June 8 at the small village of Newton in the Willows, right on the edge of the Boughton estate, where a mob destroyed the Tresham family enclosures.

Sir Edward had not followed the unpopular policy of enclosure, but he was still obliged to control the uprising. The documents relating to the surrender of the Newton rebels survive in the archives. Lady Montagu had written in a panic from London praying that her husband would 'look well to yourself', as she had heard a great army of 5,000 had gathered at Kettering. 'God knoweth what their intend is,' she wrote, but rumour had it that the men planned to go to Boughton to speak with him. Perhaps they hoped he would support their cause. The Rev. Joseph Bentham, Edward's biographer, who was a local clergyman at the time, remembers him going into the fields in Newton to negotiate with the protesters, 'without fear and danger', when 'some other justices and gentlemen dared not come near'. Edward admitted to his wife that he felt he had no choice but to have two of the rebels hanged at Kettering.

James I often came hunting in the forests of Northamptonshire. In the high summer of 1616 Edward was in attendance when he killed a buck and ordered that it be sent to old Lady Montagu. Edward's mother was 'stone blind', but the King marvelled that she was still a fine needlewoman. Edward

Elizabeth Jeffrey, Lady Montagu (d. 1611)
The 1st Lord Montagu married his first wife at Weekley in 1585. Ironically her great nephew was the notorious Judge Jeffreys, who was to deal brutally with the rebel army of the Duke of Monmouth in 1685 after the Battle of Sedgemoor

BELOW A EUROPEAN 'TURKEY RUG'
The greatest legacies of the Elizabethan luxury trade at Boughton are its four 'Turkey rugs'. Oriental carpets were imported in great numbers into Tudor England, but these are 'Occidental' carpets woven with a 'Turkish' knot. Their origin is unknown, but they may have been made in Norfolk or Antwerp. This is one of the three in the 'star' Ushak design bearing the Montagu arms. They may have been ordered by the 2nd Sir Edward to celebrate his son's marriage to Elizabeth Jeffrey in 1585. Two bear the years 1584 and 1585, making them the earliest dated European carpets in the Turkish manner

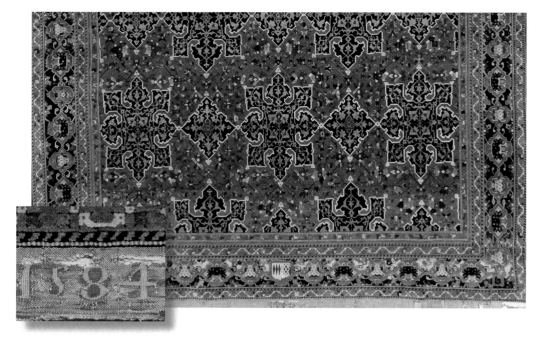

later presented the King with a handkerchief she had hemmed.

The 3rd Sir Edward was created Lord Montagu in 1621, a privilege gained as someone 'honest and faithful' to the King but helped, as was customary at the time, by his payment of £10,000, about which he complained. On the other hand, he was a generous local philanthropist, in 1611 founding the Montagu Hospital in Weekley, later known as the Almshouse, and helping to establish Weekley's Free School in 1624. He had a powerful sense of morality, and one contemporary noted that he was 'so severe and regular in his life that he was by most reckoned amongst the Puritans'.

Although critical of Charles I, Lord Montagu remained ultimately loyal, and it was the Parliamentarians who had him incarcerated in the Tower early in the Civil War. Failing health led to his release under house arrest in lodgings in the old Savoy Palace, where he died in 1644.

ABOVE LEFT *This carpet, with its distinctive 'arabesque' or 'Lotto' pattern, is one of Boughton's four Elizabethan 'Turkey rugs', copied by a European weaver from a west Anatolian prototype*

LEFT *Tapestries have been part of Boughton's interiors since Tudor times. This is one of four panels illustrating the story of Judith and Holofernes that now hang in the Secretary's Room in the Low Pavilion and the Flower Gallery Passage. They were left to the future 1st Lord Montagu by Frances Sidney, Countess of Sussex, his great-aunt, in 1588. The Countess was Queen Elizabeth's Lady of the Bedchamber and founder of Sidney Sussex College, Cambridge – Edward's brother James would lay the foundation stone and become the first Master of the college in 1596*

Above English School, 1634
Anne Crouch, Lady Montagu (1585–1648)
*Lord Montagu's third wife, daughter of John
Crouch of Cornbury, Hertfordshire. Some of her
poetry survives in the archives*

Right Follower of Hieronymus Custodis
Frances Cotton, Lady Montagu (1586–1620)
*In 1612, after his first wife's death, Lord Montagu
married the sister of his friend the antiquarian
Sir Robert Cotton, whose remarkable library
eventually formed the basis of the British Library.
She bore him two sons and a daughter. The
cockerel represents the arms of her mother's family,
the Tamworths. Her husband's Monthermer
eagle is on the left. A letter from her brother
communicated advice from their mother, who
knew she was a 'much talker' and advises
that in married life 'more will be discovered by
a seemly silence than by much prattling'*

Edward, 2nd Lord Montagu (1616–84)

The sober portrait by Robert Walker of Edward, 2nd Lord Montagu, with its black-and-white severity, sums up this most Puritan of the Montagus, who supported Parliament and Cromwell, at least until the execution of the King. This reflected in part his father's inclinations and his own education at Sidney Sussex College – the most radical of the Cambridge colleges, where Cromwell had studied. Edward's wife, Anne Winwood, whom he married in 1633, had even more extreme religious views. His father had been worried about them and insisted that she follow the Book of Common Prayer, rather than her own prayers, when she stayed at Boughton.

Edward Montagu was a Member of Parliament for Huntingdon, Cromwell's home constituency, and escorted Charles I to house arrest at Holdenby in Northamptonshire. After his father's death he was active in the House of Lords and was one of Parliament's commissioners to the Scottish army. His cousins Sir Gilbert Pickering and Sir James Harington both sat in judgement at the trial of the King, but Montagu could not reconcile himself to Charles's execution.

During the Protectorate and the Restoration, Edward's concerns lay chiefly with increasing the size of his estates, and with his children, particularly the alarming progress of his eldest son, Edward. His only daughter, Elizabeth, Lady Harvey, had a more glittering career in the court of Charles II. His second son, Ralph, built a successful career at court, made a brilliant match and created a grand London house, so Edward could reflect on the glamour and riches his children had achieved during his quiet residence at Boughton. According to John Bridges, the county historian, he deliberately avoided going to court.

ABOVE ROBERT WALKER (1599–1658)
Edward, 2nd Lord Montagu of Boughton (1616–84)
The 2nd Lord Montagu (by a painter whose other sitters included Cromwell) remained a Puritan at heart. He may have acquired the 1630s 'Acts of the Apostles' tapestries from the Earl of Pembroke's sale in the 1650s (page 90), but his hand on Boughton appears slight and he has no monument in the church. It is said that he 'lived mostly at his country seat after the Restoration, neither was it very pleasing to him that his sons engaged in the service of the court'. Letters survive about his sister-in-law upsetting him by trying to make him dance at a ball

The unfortunate Ned: the Hon. Edward Montagu (1635–65)

The 2nd Lord Montagu's elder son, Edward, or 'Ned' as he was known, completed his education with a Grand Tour of Europe in 1656–57. In a letter in the archives written from Rome in May 1656 he promises to improve himself and gives news that his cousin Walter Montagu is helping him with introductions to cardinals. This was anything but good news to his father, with his Puritan leanings, for Walter was a dangerous figure, a Catholic spy and chaplain to the Dowager Queen, Henrietta Maria. It was rumoured that Ned came back from Rome a Catholic, which would have been a complete abhorrence. He further upset his father with his unsuitable marital ambitions, his growing debts and his involvement in a duel in 1658, which led to him being summoned before Cromwell.

For a time things took a turn for the better with the Restoration of Charles II. According to Samuel Pepys, Ned had acted as an intermediary between his cousin Admiral Edward Montagu, the head of the Commonwealth's navy, and the exiled King. Now he was elected MP for Sandwich and gained a position at court as Master of the Queen's Horse. In 1663 the King expressed his favour towards him and his younger brother, Ralph, to their father, and even engineered a reconciliation between father and son.

Unfortunately, Ned then angered the King by being too forward with the Queen, Catherine of Braganza, by squeezing her hand, according to Lord Clarendon. He was dismissed, and his post went to brother Ralph. Pepys, who did not much like Edward, recorded his fall on May 20, 1664: 'Mr Edward Montagu is turned out of

ABOVE ENGLISH SCHOOL, C.1700
The Hon. Edward Montagu (1635–65)
'Ned' Montagu, the 2nd Lord Montagu's heir and Master of the Queen's Horse, was thrown out of Charles II's court for squeezing the Queen's hand

the court, not to return again. His fault, I perceive, was his pride, and most of all, his affecting to be great with the Queen and it seems indeed he had more of her ear than anybody else.'

Ned turned again to his cousin Admiral Montagu, now 1st Earl of Sandwich, and volunteered to serve on one of his ships. His last letter to his father before he set sail, to be opened only after his death, survives in the archives. In it he hopes that 'my repentance and the many hearty submissions I have made to you will have wiped away all your displeasure', adding that he does not want those who have lent him money to suffer. He concludes, 'I have nothing to add but to assure Your Lordship that my repentance is real and that it [is] in my heart.' A list of his debtors follows, including a draper at Oundle and three of his servants for three years' wages. The letter is

annotated by Ralph. 'All these debts and others very considerable not mentioned in this paper I paid before my marriage with the Countess of Northumberland out of kindness and respect to my brother's memory and for the honour of the family, out of the advantages I had raised by my own industry without troubling my father or bringing any encumbrance upon the lands or estate that was to descend to me.' Ned was killed in action fighting the Dutch in a naval battle at Bergen on August 3, 1665.

Elizabeth, Lady Harvey, 'the English Fox' (1639–1702)

The 2nd Lord Montagu's only daughter, Elizabeth (Betty), Lady Harvey, had an equally controversial, if more glittering and enduring, career in the court circles of Charles II and subsequent monarchs. Her husband, Daniel, who was knighted shortly after the King's return from exile, was posted to Constantinople as Ambassador to the Ottoman Empire in 1668, dying there four years later. Lady Harvey accompanied him only briefly and preferred a life moving between London and Paris. There she delighted in the part she could play in the intrigues involving Charles II's beloved sister Henrietta ('Minette'), who was married to Louis XIV's brother the Duc d'Orléans, and various of the King's mistresses. According to the writer Charles de Saint-Évremond, she had a great but subtle influence in politics.

Renowned as a wit and a source of gossip, she charmed intellectuals such as Jean de la Fontaine, the famed French writer of fables, one of which, *Le Renard Anglais* (*The English Fox*), he dedicated to her – '*A Madame Harvey*'. Lavish in its praise, it has the first line '*Le bon coeur est chez vous compagnon du bon sens*' ('A good heart is in you companion to good sense'). Always close to her surviving brother, Ralph, Elizabeth died in 1702.

Power and influence

Three very different men held the title of Duke of Montagu. Between them they helped to transform Boughton in the 17th and 18th centuries, introducing dramatic architecture, noble monuments and glorious art

Ralph, 1st Duke of Montagu (1638–1709)

U ntil his brother Ned's dismissal from court and demise in 1665, Ralph Montagu's prospects were limited. Yet four decades later, by the time of his own death in 1709, his legacy makes him without doubt the single most significant individual in the story of Boughton.

Ralph is a difficult ancestor to write about. The glory and diversity of that architectural and cultural legacy, the traits of kindness and generosity to family and friends, his evident love of his first wife and his children, his cultivating of writers and musicians, his unquenchable enthusiasm for life, weigh immensely in the balance.

Against all this, unfortunately, is the inescapable evidence of a man wholly

OPPOSITE BENEDETTO GENNARI (1633–1715)
Ralph, 1st Duke of Montagu (1638–1709)
'Mr Montagu' at the height of his political influence as Ambassador to Louis XIV
RIGHT SIR PETER LELY (1618–80)
Elizabeth Wriothesley, Countess of Northumberland (d.1690), late 1660s
Granddaughter of Shakespeare's patron the 3rd Earl of Southampton, Ralph's first wife was greatly loved

unscrupulous and devious, tireless in the pursuit of personal interest, be it the advancement of his fortune, the accumulation of honours or the seduction of yet another mistress. The dark and jowly features captured in Benedetto Gennari's portrait (page 19) reinforce the impression of a man who will brook no opposition.

One explanation, though no excuse, is that he was a man of his times. The corruption and licentiousness that stained the politics of Charles II's reign, and that of his counterpart Louis XIV across the Channel, are hard to exaggerate. Bribery was the common currency. Ralph was at the heart of the process of buying influence and being bought, thanks to twice holding the appointment of English Ambassador to France between 1669 and 1678. This involved periodic lengthy residences on the Continent, which were supplemented by periods of exile to escape the claws of an outraged King Charles.

The most graphic illustration in Ralph's case was his engineering of the downfall in 1678 of the King's leading minister, the Lord Treasurer, Danby, who, as he revealed in the House of Commons, had solicited on Charles's behalf huge payments from Louis XIV in return for England staying neutral in the Continental wars then raging. This was in spite of Parliament having voted money shortly before for the very purpose of supporting the Protestant William of Orange against the French. Ralph was fortunate that his receipt of over 100,000 livres of French gold for undertaking this treacherous act was overlooked in the outcry, initially at least.

The years that followed were dominated by trials of strength between Charles and a series of elected parliaments known as the Exclusion Crisis and focusing on the question of succession. Should the King's Catholic brother, James, Duke of York, be barred from the throne in favour of his eldest but illegitimate son the

Protestant Duke of Monmouth? Ralph was deeply involved in the scheming around the latter. He was fortunate not to meet his end on the scaffold, as his brother-in-law William, Lord Russell, did in 1683, when he was convicted of treason after the Rye House Plot to assassinate Charles and James.

In these difficult times any offices of state he held were removed, and it was only after the Glorious Revolution of 1688 and the enthronement of William of Orange and his wife Mary in 1689 that he advanced up the peerage, receiving the earldom for which he had long pleaded on behalf of his father. The dukedom came in 1705, shortly after his son John married Mary Churchill, daughter of the great Duke of Marlborough and his powerful wife Sarah. The latter appears to have engineered the title from Queen Anne for the sake of her new son-in-law, but even she was unable to ensure the Order of the Garter, which Ralph now coveted as the ultimate accolade.

The complications of Ralph's romantic life were a match for, and often intertwined with, his political life. That he almost certainly seduced Anne, Countess of Sussex, the King's 18-year-old daughter by Barbara Castlemaine, Duchess of Cleveland, while she was notionally staying in a convent near Paris in 1677, gives a flavour of his dangerously impulsive behaviour. Earlier, in 1673, his successful pursuit of his first wife, Elizabeth Wriothesley, the young widowed Countess of Northumberland, had equally irritated the King, who had his eye on her for his illegitimate son the future Duke of Grafton. When challenged by the King to give the reason for her choice, she coolly replied, 'The Same that Your Majesty saw in him to choose him for an Ambassador.'

Immensely wealthy, with £6,000 a year and property in London from her father, the Earl of Southampton, Elizabeth took much wooing, fearful that remarriage would lose

Above Circle of Benedetto Gennari
Hortense Mancini, Duchesse de Mazarin (1646–90)
This portrait of one of Ralph's mistresses, the influential niece of France's Minister of Finance, hung in his bedroom until his death. Today it hangs in the Fourth State Room (page 70)

Top right William Sherwin (1645–1711)
Elizabeth, Duchess of Albemarle and Montagu (1654–1734)
The 'Mad Duchess' inherited her first husband's fortune and was convinced the Emperor of China wanted her hand in marriage. The newly widowed Ralph Montagu obliged by dressing the part
Right and above right *Montagu House, Bloomsbury, as Ralph rebuilt it in 1686. 'The grandest house built in London in the second half of the 17th century' became the British Museum in 1759. George Scharf's drawing shows giraffes on the Great Staircase before its demolition in 1845. The Montagu legacy survives in local street names*

her the guardianship of Lady Betty Percy, her young daughter by her first marriage. Once won over, however, she proved an extraordinarily loyal and forgiving spouse, who bore Ralph a daughter and three sons, the birth of the last of whom, John, in 1790 was to be followed shortly afterwards by her own death. The closeness of the family was much remarked on, and they were brought closer by the death of their eldest son in 1687 at the age of eight, after which for a time they

left London together, unable to remain where the tragedy had occurred.

Elizabeth's death brought Ralph not only great unhappiness but a degree of financial insecurity. It was with this in mind that he set about his next conquest, that of the 38-year-old widow Elizabeth, Duchess of Albemarle, wealthy not only through her late husband but through her father, the Duke of Newcastle. Ralph's success was to be the source of much legal dispute and ribald mockery but also of a substantial fortune. By every account the poor lady was mad, and she had asserted that she would only marry the Emperor of China. With Ralph thus disguised, she gave her consent, though her capacity to consent was challenged in court. She spent the rest of their married life waited on as befits an empress but in close confinement, while

the charade was maintained.

Ralph's father, the 2nd Lord Montagu, died early in 1684, and one feels that the last quarter-century of Ralph's life reflected a change of emphasis. The legacy of his politicking still unavoidably played a part. Following his brother-in-law Lord Russell's involvement in the Rye House Plot in 1683, he went into exile in the south of France. He was allowed to return in 1686 and, in 1688, played a relatively small part in the Glorious Revolution, which saw James II exiled in favour of William and Mary, but there is a feeling that increasingly he was on the margins of the political world.

In 1689 he did, however, have restored to him the office of Master of the Great Wardrobe, the sinecure that gave responsibility for overseeing the furnishing of the Royal Palaces. He had obtained this first in 1671, then been stripped of it in 1685. The post brought a considerable revenue stream for the incumbent, and guides us in a sense to what was to command ever more of his interest and time: the creation of palatial houses of remarkable beauty, filled with paintings and decorative arts in the finest taste.

Evidence of this passion was clear well before he came into his own inheritance. He had acquired the Mortlake tapestry workshops from his sister in 1674, and in 1675 Robert Hooke had designed for him the first Montagu House in Bloomsbury, described by John Evelyn as 'somewhat after the French, nobly furnished and fine'.

When disaster struck eight years later – the house burnt to the ground while let to the Earl of Devonshire – Ralph scarcely paused before embarking on a rebuilding programme that made it grander than ever, with wonderful painted interiors that could still be admired a century later, by which time it was the home of the British

The North Prospect of MOUNTAGUE HOUSE.

Freemasons… the eclectic list goes on and on. Nor did he neglect his inheritance.

Known especially for his works in the landscape – he earned the nickname John the Planter for the many miles of avenues he planted – he also reordered parts of Boughton and, most importantly, organised the building of a new Montagu House by the architect Henry Flitcroft on the banks of the Thames near Whitehall (page 136). The family moved into it in 1733.

In many of his undertakings Duke John was greatly stimulated by his close friend the Reverend William Stukeley, antiquarian and early explorer of Stonehenge, for whom he eventually organised a living at St George the Martyr in Bloomsbury in 1747. Few of Stukeley's own ideas were translated into reality – the Gothic-style bridge for the park at Boughton (opposite) and the Mausoleum on the Mount (page 214) got little further than the drawing board – but there was no doubt that this clever if irritating individual was a great ally to the Duke when needed.

Duke John shared Stukeley's love of antiquarianism, local history and archaeology, to which the heraldic decoration and recycling of old architectural features all through Boughton stand in testimony. He was ahead of fashion in his interest in reviving Gothic architecture: he toyed with designs for castles and wanted to restore his medieval hall. He did repair the Eleanor Cross in Geddington and Barnwell Castle. Uniting heraldry and medieval history, he was also instrumental in reviving the Order of the Bath in 1725. The Great Mastership of the Order was created for him by the King so that John could collect fees and to a degree profit from the power that admittance to the order would confer. He even proposed an order for the American colonies and one for women. *Writhe's Garter Book*, one of the great treasures of the archives, depicts the ceremonies a medieval knight went through

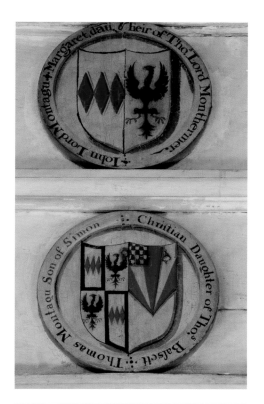

to enter the Order. The book had its origins with John's mother's ancestors.

It was Stukeley who recorded so well John's great kindness to animals. According to the Boughton archives, this extended to a retired and toothless circus lion: the Duke issued the most precise instructions regarding its diet, and on general measures for its safety to ensure that it did not drown in the park canals. In Stukeley's biography it is noted that 'he would have no cattle or horses killed but brought to end their days peacefully in a special paddock while he was surrounded by dogs, the ugliest of which he favoured because no one else would be kind to it.' The Duke even made this clear in his will, which concluded, 'I do further will that none of my horses, dogs, cats or other living animals that I shall be possessed of at the time of my decease… shall be sold, given away or otherwise disposed of but that all such my horses, dogs, cats and other living animals shall be fed, kept and maintained in and upon some part of my honors, manors, messages, lands, tenements or hereditaments hereby devised until they shall die a natural death.'

As far as his own demise was concerned, he was less precise. As it turned out, thanks to his younger daughter, Mary, this was a further area in which, surprisingly, he was to outdo his father – the other being his receipt of the Order of the Garter in 1718. Having been made his heiress, she ensured that neither her father nor her mother would be forgotten, by commissioning two of the finest monuments undertaken by Louis-François Roubiliac, which stand to this day in Warkton's church (page 224) as a glorious reminder of a good and kind man.

As a distinguished contemporary, Lord Hailes, pointed out, 'His vast benevolence of soul is not recorded by Pope; but it will be remembered while there is any tradition of human kindness and charity in England.'

Lady Mary Montagu, Duchess of Montagu (1712–75), and George, 3rd Duke of Montagu (1712–90)

Duke John was deeply concerned with ancestry and titles, as his father had been, and it was therefore a sad irony that his three sons all died in infancy, leaving two daughters, Isabella and Mary. The elder, Isabella, was beautiful, headstrong and dangerous. Her first marriage, to the Duke of Manchester in 1723, was tinged with scandal. When she initially rejected him, he tried to kill himself. Lord Hervey described them as 'the she tiger and the jack ass'. The Earl of Scarborough, who should have been her second husband, did kill himself the day before their wedding. Eventually, in 1743, she found love with an Irishman, Edward

importance. The engagement showed every sign of being founded on genuine affection, and correspondence reveals the pleasure it gave to both families. It is only with the benefit of hindsight that we sense that the sickly disposition of Elizabeth's brother, John, would lead to a life curtailed and to her becoming one of the great heiresses of the day. With his death three years later, all the ambitions of Ralph, John and George to perpetuate the Montagu dukedom came finally to naught, although Elizabeth and Henry at least adopted the family surname of Montagu Scott for their children.

Boughton fades from the picture at this point, as their lives were firmly rooted in Scotland, on Henry's extensive estates, a choice heavily influenced by the advice of his eminent tutor and lifelong friend, the economist Adam Smith, who held firm views on the responsibilities of great landowners. After the death of Elizabeth's father in 1790, Montagu House in Whitehall became their principal London residence, and other Montagu properties on the Thames, at Richmond and further upstream at Ditton, near Datchet, were also used. There was no shortage of substantial houses, particularly after her husband inherited the Douglas title of Duke of Queensberry along with land and a great castle, Drumlanrig, in Dumfriesshire.

However, Elizabeth appears to have retained a keen sense of her Northamptonshire links. She was widely admired for her charitable works in the area and left instructions that she should be buried at St Edmund's, Warkton, alongside her mother and Montagu grandparents on her death, which occurred in 1827. The rather pedestrian sculpture of her by Thomas Campbell (page 225) belies a remarkable and energetic character who was an important patron of music, among other things. Boughton's outstanding music archive owes a great deal to her.

Boughton reawakens

Rarely visited for 150 years, Boughton was saved from overuse and the temptations of a Victorian makeover; in the 20th century, a gentler rediscovery began

Henry, Elizabeth's husband, died in 1812 and was succeeded as 4th Duke of Buccleuch and 6th Duke of Queensberry by their son Charles. A man of gentle humour and charm, he suffered from ill health and died in 1819, leaving his son Walter Francis to become the 5th Duke as a boy of 12.

His mother having died a few years earlier, the young man's upbringing was very much in the hands of two guardians, one the writer Sir Walter Scott, a kinsman and close friend of the family, the other his uncle Henry (Charles's brother). Through his mother, Elizabeth, Henry had been able to inherit the

A 1906 view of the West Front across the dried-up Broad Water. The field in front of the house was traditionally known as the 'Drip Pan'

one surviving Montagu peerage, that of Lord Montagu of Boughton, with which the family had started two centuries before and which could pass through the female line. He lived at Ditton, on the Thames, where he collected a remarkable library. Sadly, he died without children, so that title also finally disappeared in 1845.

Walter Francis married Charlotte Anne Thynne, daughter of the Marquess of Bath, in 1829. They both had prodigious energy and together substantially expanded Bowhill, the home nearest to the 12th-century origins of the Scott family in the Scottish Borders, as well as rebuilding Montagu House in London. Their collecting passions are particularly illustrated at Boughton in the French furniture, and in the Sèvres porcelain accumulated over a short period early in their married life.

They do not appear to have spent much time at Boughton, or indeed at Palace House, Beaulieu, near Southampton, another Montagu property, which had been part of Duke Ralph's inheritance from his mother, a daughter of the Earl of Southampton. However, their second son, also Henry, did occupy Palace House, particularly after he became a Member of Parliament for a Hampshire constituency. When he retired in 1885 he was created the 1st Lord Montagu of Beaulieu, and the estate there, as well as the one at Ditton, was passed to him along with parts of the art collection. Beaulieu is now the home of Ralph, 4th Lord Montagu of Beaulieu, and is famous for its remarkable National Motor Museum.

At about the same time a part of Boughton known as the Dower House was being occupied by Henry's brother Admiral Lord Charles Montagu Douglas Scott, who made it a family home for his wife, Ada Ryan, and their two children, Charles and David. Ada was an Australian whom he had married in Sydney in 1883 (sister of the celebrated botanical artist Marian Ellis, Mrs Charles Rowan). The Admiral had been entrusted with the care of the Prince of Wales and Prince George when they sailed round the world in HMS *Bacchante* in 1879–82 and he was subsequently made Commander-in-Chief of the Australian Station (1889–92) and the Plymouth Station (1900–04). The Dower House was to be their home until his death in 1911, and his son David was to occupy it until his own death in 1986.

This branch of the family is warmly remembered as perhaps the first in Boughton's history to make it a year-round home. The main building was dilapidated and David used to recount how as a boy he kept and flew his hawks in the Great Hall. The Dower House became a place of special memories for all who visited it, filled with a famous collection of Victorian paintings bought for a few pounds before they became fashionable, and an eclectic mix of fascinating objects. The garden created by David from the 1920s onward was legendary, and its fame grew with his second wife, the well-known horticulturalist and photographer Valerie Finnis.

The reoccupation of Boughton by the principal branch of the family was a slow process

ABOVE *Bowhill in Scotland, the Borders home of the Scotts of Buccleuch, where the Montagu legacy includes Mortlake tapestries of Mantegna's 'Triumphs of Caesar' and Lord Monthermer's Italian vedute*
LEFT *William Burn, who enlarged Bowhill, rebuilt Montagu House in Whitehall for the 5th Duke in 1862*
BELOW LEFT *Admiral Charles Scott as a child*
BELOW *The 3rd Duchess of Montagu's vlla at Richmond, where she kept her blanc-de-chine figurines*
OPPOSITE *Boughton in 1906 (top) and the 1860s*

Boughton House. Kettering

that began with William, the 6th Duke, and his wife, Louisa Jane. Just how run-down Boughton had become is apparent in the photographs taken for *Country Life* in 1909.

The greatest threat had been the 'Gothic zeal' of the Victorian architect Sir Arthur Blomfield, who wished to turn the Great Hall from 'doubtful classical into fine Gothic'. A grandson of the 5th Duke's recalled him saying that as soon as Blomfield 'drove up to the front door the house began to shake'. He remembered how he 'wrenched the panelling and much excellent plaster work off the walls of the Great Hall, in order to see what lay behind'. Duke Ralph's scheme of decoration had been 'on the gloomy side' but 'decidedly impressive'.

Attempts to make Boughton habitable focused on the South and West Fronts, where

sitting and dining rooms as well as bedrooms were created. Photograph albums show happy family groupings and various of their children and grandchildren, in particular Princess Alice, Duchess of Gloucester, who wrote affectionately of the magic of Boughton. They even left their mark in cartoon graffiti hidden by the tapestries in the night nursery.

It was the 8th Duke and his wife, Mollie, however, who brought the house forward in leaps and bounds. Modern bathrooms were installed. The renowned interior decorator John Fowler was called in. Fowler advised on the refurbishment of the elegant Drawing Room with its new fireplace, removed from another Montagu house, and the banishment of the Victorian clutter. Even then the house was only occupied for a few brief summer months, but it made up for the rest of the year with a flow of glamorous and amusing house parties.

The present Duke's parents, Johnnie, the 9th Duke, and his wife Jane, continued the same pattern, and now it seems hard to imagine such a house remaining virtually dormant for decades on end.

Lady's Walk. Boughton

FAR LEFT *William, 6th Duke of Buccleuch, in 1906 (left), the first in three generations to make a home of Boughton*
ABOVE *Three of his children, Francis, Constance and Katharine, in 1887*
LEFT *Much-admired stately limes, 1889*
TOP *A garden party at Montagu House in 1894 using the Chinese Pavilion*

RIGHT *The Great Hall in 'Country Life', 1909. Thanks to the architect Sir Arthur Blomfield's 'Gothic zeal', it had long been derelict. It was repanelled in 1911*
TOP RIGHT *Blomfield felt he'd discovered structural weakness in the Unfinished Wing, bracing it with great oak beams that were removed in 1885*

The Buccleuch family albums *Between the Thirties and the Sixties, Boughton returns to life with a flourish as*

CLOCKWISE FROM LEFT *Prime Minister Neville Chamberlain's rally, July 1938; Lord Harewood and Winston Churchill; Douglas Fairbanks and HRH the Duchess of Kent; Ian Gilmour (right), who married the 9th Duke's sister Caroline, with publisher Hamish Hamilton and his wife; Queen Mary and former Prime Minister Stanley Baldwin (far right) in 1938, entertained by the 8th Duke*

a stage set for glamorous gatherings of politicians, film stars, artists and royalty…

CLOCKWISE FROM LEFT
The film star Ava Gardner outside the West Front (1955); lunch in the Great Hall, with the Chinese screen visible on the right (1954); Mollie, 8th Duchess, pouring tea (1952); Aimée de Heeren, seen with Doria Scott and daughter Henrietta, 'carried gaiety with her like a fan', according to Vogue editor Bettina Ballard (1954); Nancy Lancaster, owner of the firm of interior decorators Sibyl Colefax & John Fowler, with Audrey Pleydell Bouverie (1953)

... and a backdrop for country-house weekends, with friends and family lazing and larking around on sunny summer days

William   hudo

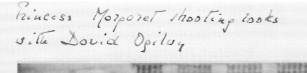

Princess Margaret shooting rooks with David Ogilvy

The Result

FAR LEFT, FROM TOP *Playwright William Douglas Home with Ludovic Kennedy; the party gravitates to the urn in the Fish Court after lunch (1954)*
LEFT *The future Earl of Airlie with Princess Margaret (top); the 8th Duke with Queen Elizabeth the Queen Mother (1954)*
BELOW *The violinist Yehudi Menuhin plays croquet (1953); photographer Cecil Beaton (1952)*
OPPOSITE, CLOCKWISE FROM TOP LEFT *The newly married Jane, Countess of Dalkeith; the Queen Mother and Princess Margaret; the present Duke and Duchess on their engagement, by Valerie Finnis; Cecil Beaton draws the tea kettle; the 8th Duke and Raine Legge; the future 9th Duke and sisters Caroline and Elizabeth*

Take the grand tour

A journey through Boughton in all its guises, from its imposing French façade and bucolic parkland to its

Boughton is many houses and many landscapes in one, as becomes clear from a walk round the outside. Ralph, 1st Duke of Montagu, wanted it to look imposing, and as you arrive through gentle English parkland with grazing sheep, the contrast accentuates the grandeur. The principal entrance, the North Front (previous pages), can even look forbidding, as it catches sunlight only briefly on summer evenings.

Slide round the corner to the West Front (below) and by contrast you might be blinking in strong midday sun, reflected off the creamy yellow of the Weldon stone, which gradually mellows and warms as the

day goes on. The West Front continues the three-storeyed French formality of the North Front but quickly steps down to two, capped with a roof-level balustrade. It is simpler, without the rusticated stonework, and is garlanded in wisteria; above it soars a forest of chimneys.

Instead of the immediacy of the lake known as the Grand Etang, which magically reflects the North Front on a still day, the western vista opens to a huge expanse of grass, edged with a stately avenue of lime trees running to the horizon across the Broad Water, another lake in the distance.

Again the mood changes as you turn the corner to the South Side (page 158). A rise

in the ground, through a very English rose garden to the terrace beside the Lily Pond, gives a view down to higgledy-piggledy rooflines on different levels and running in different directions. The chimneys, sticking up like pencils, seem even taller. As the gaze shifts from left to right, stone gives way to a rich, rusty brick, although some degree of unity is provided by the Collyweston slates that blanket a hectare of roof.

The public face of the house greeting the visitor, including the Stables, may be stone, but humbler brick is the order of the day behind the scenes. By the time you reach the Stable Yard, passing the jumble of buildings that made a great house self-sufficient – the laundry, the carpenters' workshops, the brewhouse – brick has taken over.

Embraced within it all are four separate courtyards, further houses within one house, each very different in character. An attic vantage point can lead the eye from serene white borders in the Fish Court to the Clock Court's herbs, and to vivid colour in the Rose Garden beyond.

PREVIOUS PAGES *The palatial North Front, inspired by Versailles. The principal entrance to the house is behind the arched Colonnade on the right. The lake, an acre of water known since the 17th century as the Grand Etang, was restored in 2014* LEFT *The West Front seen across the Broad Water. This 1720s façade of creamy Weldon stone meets the the 1st Duke's 1690s French palace on the far left. The old Tudor manor house lies behind*

remodelled Tudor interiors and labyrinth of courtyards

Boughton's North Front stretches in a broad panorama from the Stables (on the left) to the principal entrance, behind the arches of Ralph Montagu's 'English Versailles', with its twin wings (in the foreground). The West Front (on the right) conceals the old Tudor house

THE NORTH FRONT, 48
This grand entrance front was begun by Ralph, 1st Duke of Montagu, in the 1690s. The architect is unknown, but the Huguenot Daniel Marot, who worked at Hampton Court Palace, probably played a part. The entrance is behind the arched Colonnade, above which are Ralph's splendid State Rooms

THE WORKING HOUSE, 170
Daily life still revolves around the Tudor kitchen. A maze of unsuspected courtyards leads to the old servants' halls, and hidden staircases lead to the atmospheric attics, with their garret storerooms and simple bedrooms

THE STABLES, 192
Finished in 1705, this block, with its arch and cupola, was the final element in Duke Ralph's transformation of Boughton. It extends the North Front to form a distinctly Parisian square, which was once paved. The 1830 Buccleuch State Coach is still kept here

THE SOUTH SIDE, 158
Once the site of the Tudor chapel, this was converted by the 2nd Duke into living quarters in 1741–43, and filled with its distinctive painted panelling. The White Drawing Room upstairs looks out over the Rose Garden

THE DOWER HOUSE, 192
Once the Laundry, this became home to Elizabeth Montagu, Dowager 3rd Duchess of Buccleuch, and was lived in most recently by Sir David Scott, a cousin of the Duke, and his wife the horticulturalist Valerie Finnis, who created a famous garden here

THE NORTHEAST PAVILION, 92
One of the two wings, the Unfinished Wing, as it is known, is a shell with bare rafters inside – time and money ran out. It now houses the Chinese Pavilion and one of England's oldest billiard tables

THE STATE ROOMS, 54
The Great Apartment, built for formal entertainment, culminating in a Bedchamber for the King. It remains unaltered after three centuries

THE NORTHWEST PAVILION, 76
Duke Ralph built these oak-panelled private apartments for himself and his wife. They occupy two floors, known as the Low and High Pavilions

THE FISH COURT AND GREAT AND LITTLE HALLS, 96
The Tudor halls were kept when Duke Ralph built his North Front, but he transformed them with splendid painted ceilings and tall windows

THE WEST FRONT, 126
In contrast to the North Front, intimate rooms full of surprises occupy two floors of the west wing of the Tudor manor house. These include Duke John's Library, the Boudoir, the Loggia, the Flower Gallery and the Nursery

THE NORTH FRONT
Duke Ralph's vision

This grand statement, distinguished by its twin 'Pavilions' and ceremonial parade of State Rooms known as the Great Apartment, was designed to introduce the majesty of Versailles to the Northamptonshire countryside

The French pedigree of Boughton's North Front, which greets the arriving visitor, is obvious. The mansard roofs and dormer windows, the pilasters and rustication of the stonework, the Colonnade – all to be found at the time in a Parisian *hôtel*, or town house – are reminiscent, as was long ago pointed out, not so much of Versailles as of its imposing stables.

The architectural historian Gervase Jackson-Stops revealed close parallels with designs by the Huguenot émigré Daniel Marot (1661–1752), particularly in the two projecting wings, or 'Pavilions'. Marot had escaped from France to work for William of Orange, the future William III of England, at his palace of Het Loo in the Netherlands, and he and Ralph Montagu possibly met there. They were to work together on the refurbishment of Hampton Court. There is nothing in the archives to link Marot to the building of Boughton, but in the absence of an identified architect it is hard not to feel that he must have been a decisive influence.

As Charles II's envoy to the court of Louis XIV, Ralph had witnessed the ceremonial involved in entertaining the grandest of guests. Started in 1685, Boughton's North Front was undertaken in essence to provide the space for doing this in his own home. Running above the Colonnade is the enfilade, or sequence of rooms, required for formality. These State Rooms, or Great Apartment, included a Dining Room, a Withdrawing Room and the State Bedchamber. In the centre of the Colonnade is the entrance the King would have used.

Ralph's magnificent private quarters were in the Northwest Pavilion (right of main picture). The Northeast Pavilion is unfinished to this day.

ABOVE *Unusually, the main entrance to Boughton is at the end of the Colonnade. Just visible on the left is the door used by William III in 1695*
LEFT *The North Front with its two 'Pavilions'. Above the arches are the windows of the State Rooms, with the State Bedchamber in the centre*

The Staircase Hall

Central to Ralph Montagu's grand plan was a magnificent staircase with ambitious trompe l'oeil murals that add to the sense of drama – but the scheme was not without its challenges

OPPOSITE *The rustication of the exterior stonework is continued in these trompe l'oeil murals by Louis Chéron. Wren's chief plasterer, Henry Doogood, prepared the walls and ceiling. The longcase clock is by William Lockin of Rugby, c.1700*
LEFT *The Colonnade, or 'Cloisters', as it is called in old accounts. The 1728 benches seen on the previous page were moved to prevent weathering (page 95)*
BELOW *Described as 'Louis XV at its wildest', the clock on the stairs, bought by the 5th Duke of Buccleuch, has an ormolu case sculpted and signed by the celebrated Jacques Caffieri (1678–1755) and a dial signed 'Balthazar Martinot à Paris', c.1740. The pedestal depicts Diana of Ephesus*

OVERLEAF *Two views from the gallery of the Staircase Hall, showing Chéron's trompe l'oeil reliefs based on the Arch of Constantine in Rome. The ceiling depicts 'Discord Throwing the Apple Amongst the Gods'. The padauk-wood chairs are said to have belonged to Catherine of Braganza*

Today's visitor must move to the right along the Colonnade, passing the busts of Roman emperors on the walls, through the high double doors at the end, directly into the Staircase Hall, commonly known as the Painted Staircase.

If Ralph Montagu's first challenge was how to incorporate the Tudor Great Hall into his building plans, a further challenge is at once revealed in the Staircase Hall, which has to accommodate the difference in ground levels between the North and West Fronts, so that wide stairs must immediately be negotiated. But far from being a problem, these add a sense of drama to the arrival. The trompe l'oeil rusticated stonework eases the transition and signals the start of the overarching decorative theme that runs through all the rooms.

This was the work of the French Huguenot painter Louis Chéron (1660–1725), who painted the ceiling and trompe l'oeil walls here and the ceilings in the State Rooms, among others – his Boughton ceilings alone cover some 6,000 square feet. It was an extraordinary tour de force by an artist sadly overshadowed by his Italian rival Antonio Verrio, to whom Ralph gave the plum job of painting the interiors of his London house.

Architectural historians have speculated that a similar, balancing staircase may have been planned for the far end of the State Room sequence, filling the space occupied by the Fifth State Room and the domestic Lime Staircase. If so, it was another of Duke Ralph's grand ideas that remained unfulfilled.

T he symmetry of Boughton's North Front is so striking that the eye and the footstep are naturally drawn to the great doorway at the centre of the Colonnade. But this is a false start, for it leads only to a dark passageway, a consequence of Ralph's laudable decision not to demolish the Tudor Great Hall, which lies behind it out of sight. In 1695 this portal served briefly as a formal entrance for William III, who was swept straight into the Great Hall.

The State Rooms

The lavishly decorated State Rooms culminating in the State Bedchamber survive as a remarkable time capsule. This suite of rooms gives a rare insight into politics and culture in the final decades of the Stuarts

When William III arrived at Boughton on October 23, 1695, the State Rooms, or Great Apartment, can barely have been ready to entertain him. It is uncertain how many of the ceilings had been painted, and even the State Bed (page 64) was somewhat cobbled together from an old French frame, rather than constructed new and in the latest fashion, as Ralph would have preferred; as so often with big building projects, time had run out. Nevertheless, the effect must have been spectacular and, 300 years on, the State Rooms remain among the most complete survivals in an English country house of a series of rooms prescribed for the grandest entertaining.

The visitor has a direct view along the whole sequence, or enfilade, which begins with the Dining Room, followed by the Withdrawing Room, then the most important room of all, the State Bedchamber; and finally the Blue Damask Room, a further, more private, sitting room. Now, as then, they are rooms of formal parade, barely altered, with only minimal electric lighting added in the last century.

The classical allegories that form the subjects of the ceiling paintings would undoubtedly have been discussed with Ralph. At times they make quite pointed political references. Thus in the Second State Room the illustration of Ovid's *Fall of Pyrenaeus* (opposite) – the tale of a tyrant possessed of an overweening sense of

self-worth, seen finally crashing to Earth and losing his crown – may well refer to the flight of King James II in 1688. Ralph was in every way a beneficiary of the Glorious Revolution, which brought William and Mary to the throne, and the direct allusion to such events would have pleased both men.

The decorative unity of the State Rooms is further enhanced in a number of ways. Throughout, there is *parquet de Versailles* flooring by Pierre Rieusset, perhaps the earliest use of this technique in England, and a costly one at that. The accounts show that more than £100,000 in today's money was spent on creating the complex pattern of

blocks, which are interlocked and pegged and which, being so special, would probably not have been covered with rugs. Today, however, they do provide an opportunity for occasional displays of pieces from Ralph's highly important Oriental rug collection.

The walls retain their original colour, now known in decorating circles as 'Boughton Drab' – a variety of khaki shades of great subtlety. The cornices are moulded, not carved, then painted in trompe l'oeil.

The first three rooms would have had crimson-covered furnishings, cushions and upholstery throughout. Some of these survive in the Second and Third State Rooms; the State Bed, in particular, meticulously restored by the Victoria and Albert Museum over many years, gives a sense of the visual impact the materials of the time, often embroidered with gold and silver thread, would have made.

Inevitably, paintings and furniture have been moved around over the centuries, but the overall impression remains as complete as that in any English country house.

ABOVE *The enfilade of State Rooms seen from the Staircase Hall. Catching the eye above the doorway is 'Angelica and Medoro with Cupid' by Lorenzo Pasinelli (1629–1700)*
OPPOSITE *Chéron's 'Fall of Pyrenaeus' in the Second State Room is based on Ovid's 'Metamorphoses'. Pyrenaeus, King of Thrace, in billowing blue-green robes, tumbles from his tower, arms and legs flailing, as the Muses look on*

The Second State Room

With the mellow reds of its Mortlake tapestries,
woven from cartoons by Raphael, the Drawing Room
would have offered a formal yet intimate retreat
from the hubbub of the Dining Room

Smaller but still formal, the Drawing Room, along with the Bedchamber next to it, most closely represents what Duke Ralph envisaged for the Great Apartment. To the right of the fireplace hangs *The Sacrifice at Lystra*, and opposite it is *The Death of Ananias* (overleaf). Both were in this room in Ralph's lifetime. They are part of a set of tapestries based on Raphael's cartoons *The Acts of the Apostles* and woven in Ralph's Mortlake factory in the 1670s and 1680s.

Pope Leo X had commissioned the cartoons in 1516, and magnificent tapestries were woven from them shortly afterwards in the Brussels workshops of Pieter van Aelst. The tapestries went back to Rome to hang in the Sistine Chapel. The cartoons were later bought by Charles I from the Gonzaga Dukes of Mantua in 1623 and now hang in the Victoria and Albert Museum.

Contemporary with the room, the William and Mary walnut chairs are covered in their original crimson velvet, faded now but still harmonising with the tones of the tapestries.

Gilt gesso furniture adds to the richness of tone. The coffer (overleaf, below the tapestry) is by James Moore (c.1670–1726), who made furniture for both Ralph and John. A bill for £47 17s in October 1722 may relate to it. The earlier centre table was made for Ralph by the Huguenot Jean Pelletier. Not to be overlooked are the pair of giltwood stools with silver-thread coverings, probably 'perquisites of office' from one of Charles II's palaces.

TOP LEFT *'The Death of Ananias'*
hangs above a gilt-gesso coffer, c.1722,
by James Moore, traditionally believed
to be another gift from the Duchess of
Marlborough. Moore was her 'oracle'
LEFT WILLIAM WISSING (1656–87)
Queen Mary II (r. 1689–94)

ABOVE EUSTACHE LE SUEUR
(1617–55)
Martyrdom of St Lawrence, 1640–41
Painted for the Church of Saint-
Germain-l'Auxerrois in Paris, this
was bought by the 3rd Duke in 1770
OPPOSITE *Raphael's stricken Ananias*

The Third State Room

The State Bedchamber, with its original State Bed topped with fantasy ostrich plumes, and Venus beckoning from the ceiling, was a fitting stage for the ritual stately progress to bed

This was a room for the privileged few, perhaps half a dozen close courtiers and friends, who were to be afforded the honour of witnessing the King's toilette. It is unlikely the King actually spent the night at Boughton, although he 'was splendidly entertained' here.

The Boughton State Bed was given by the present Duke's great-grandfather to the Victoria and Albert Museum in 1916. After nearly 90 years, and having benefited from over 6,000 hours of painstaking restoration, it has been loaned back to the house to assume its original place once again. The richness of the crimson damask hangings with gold brocading, and the flamboyance of the original silvered finials with ostrich and egret feathers, remind us how breathtakingly bold these rooms must have been when they were new.

The chairs and materials became increasingly lavish as visitors progressed towards the State Bedchamber, simple chairs with rush seats and plain damask cushions in the Dining Room giving way to velvet and gold-brocaded damask in the Drawing Room and culminating in the luxurious crimson silk of the bed itself. Between the windows is a mirror of Portuguese ebony and below that another marquetry table by Daniel Marot.

The allegory about infidelity in the ceiling painting by Louis Chéron – *Vulcan Catching Mars and Venus in His Net* – would no doubt have been carefully chosen.

THE STATE BEDCHAMBER
The French upholsterer Francis Lapiere (1653–1714) was asked to dismantle the 'Crimson gold flowered bed' at Montagu House and reassemble it at Boughton in 1704. Donated to the Victoria and Albert Museum during the First World War, it returned to the house on loan in 2005

The Mortlake tapestries here were again woven from Raphael's 'Acts of the Apostles' cartoons in the 1670s–80s. Behind the bed hangs 'The Healing of the Lame Man' and on the west wall is 'St Paul Preaching'

The carpet is one of two small 'Polonaise' silk rugs woven in Isfahan in the early 17th century. Unusually, it retains its vivid colours

TOP LEFT *One of the State Bed's exotic ostrich-plume finials*
ABOVE *The tapestry in the corner is 'The Miraculous Draught of Fishes', from Raphael's cartoon. Above the fireplace is a portrait after Van Dyck of Charles II as a boy, and above the door, Duke*

Ralph's stepdaughter, Lady Elizabeth Percy, painted c.1679–80 by Benedetto Gennari
ABOVE RIGHT *An ideal foil for paintings and tapestries, the 'Boughton Drab' paintwork has aged well in the north-facing State Rooms. The portrait of*

Edward VI (1537–53) as a child hangs above a Louis XIV marriage casket, or 'coffre de toilette', inlaid with tortoiseshell and brass, one of three at Boughton attributed to André-Charles Boulle

OPPOSITE *'Vulcan Catching Mars and Venus in His Net'. Chéron's four State Room ceilings were designed to be seen first from the western door to each room. Here he introduces a clever artistic trick. As the viewer moves across the room, Venus appears to sit up as if in welcome*

The Fourth State Room

Once known as the 'Blew Damask Room', the last room in the original grand parade is a complete contrast to the earlier State Rooms. Raphael's Apostles give way to festive villagers in a rural Arcadia, and flame-stitch embroidery replaces the vibrant crimson damask

This might have been a daytime room of business for the King or a principal guest as well as a private dressing room where he could prepare for the official *levée*. Compared with the formal Drawing Room (the Second State Room), it was a retreat away from the scrutiny of his courtly circle. A secret door behind one of the tapestries leads to what is now known as the State Bedroom, not a state room, but the sanctuary where the King would actually have slept had he stayed.

The 1697 inventory called it the 'Blew Damask Room'. By 1709, it was simply the 'Blue Room'. In contrast to the crimson and tapestries of the previous rooms, blue damask with gold tassels was probably used for the wall hangings and curtains. A flavour of the scheme can be had from the armchair and stool in the Fifth State Room (page 74).

For many years, the blue hangings have been replaced by 17th-century French tapestries depicting the pastoral story of *The Loves of Gombaut and Macée*, fondly known in the family as 'Gumboot and Messy'. Seven of the eight original tapestries are at Boughton, the only near-complete set to survive.

The eye-catching flame-stitch coverings of the contemporary William and Mary sofas and chairs harmonise with the tapestries. The pattern is described sometimes as Hungarian, sometimes as Florentine.

This room, unlike others, has a painted

The two tapestries are from the French series 'The Loves of Gombaut and Macée'. 'La Danse' (left) shows shepherds and shepherdesses at the age of 20. In 'La Soupe' (right), children, supposedly aged 10, eat soup and catch butterflies

The silk 'Polonaise' rug, now faded, was woven in Isfahan, c.1600. The porcelain on the console table (centre) includes Savona maiolica, c.1700, Delft dishes dated 1742, and 18th-century English Delft

Ralph's monogram is inscribed on the pendulum window of the clock in the corner. The case, inlaid with tortoiseshell and brass, is by André-Charles Boulle, 1690–95

architrave featuring the 'RM' monogram of Ralph Montagu. The ceiling portrays *Jupiter Restraining Arcas from Shooting at the Bear*.

Above the fireplace hangs the favourite niece of Cardinal Mazarin, Hortense Mancini, Duchesse de Mazarin (1646–99) (page 20). Ralph hoped to tempt Charles II to take her as a mistress but she ended up as Ralph's friend and lover instead. This painting is known to have hung in his bedroom at Montagu House.

ABOVE *In the fourth ceiling of the series by Chéron, Jupiter attempts to restrain Arcas from shooting his mother, Callisto, who has been turned into a bear by the jealous Diana. They appear among the signs of the Zodiac, with Callisto as the Great Bear* RIGHT *The oyster-veneered walnut table in the middle of the room is by Daniel Marot. The flame-stitch chair coverings are contemporary. Behind the tapestry of 'The Betrothal of Gombaut and Macée' in the corner is a secret door to the room where the King would actually have slept*

The Fifth State Room

This is a room of compromise, once intended as a staircase. It derives its atmosphere from the tall, angled fireplace and the permanently locked door that would have led to the unfinished Northeast Pavilion

The Fifth State Room at the east end of the Great Apartment differs from the others, with its plain floorboards. It was intended originally to form part of a staircase leading to the upper suite in the Northeast Pavilion, the closed door to which is in the north wall. In the 19th century the room was used as the billiard room. In 1709 it was simply 'the first room in the Great Apartment'.

The corner fireplace carries more blanc de chine and is set at an oblique angle in order to share the chimney with the fireplace of the Fourth State Room. The large armchair and stool by the window (overleaf) are upholstered in the blue damask embroidered with metallic thread that would have been such a striking feature of the Fourth State Room. The giltwood chairs and winged settee (left) are William and Mary but have later coverings.

Next to the fireplace hangs a portrait of the second Sir Edward Montagu (page 10). Above him, his father, the first Sir Edward, who completed the purchase of Boughton in 1536, sits at his desk looking glum, which perhaps owes something to the time he spent in the Tower for his role as one of the drafters of the will of the short-lived Edward VI. This identified the ill-fated Lady Jane Grey as his successor, rather than Mary, who duly became queen in 1553. A written testimony survives in the archives.

Gombaut and Macée seem to be absorbed in a game of croquet or golf (here called

boules) in the tapestry on the fireplace wall. The Mortlake tapestry on the facing wall, *The Death of Sapphira* (overleaf), is from the earlier of the two *Acts of the Apostles* sets at Boughton, woven in 1638–40 (see page 90). Ananias and his wife, Sapphira, suffered divine retribution for not sharing their wealth with their early Christian brothers.

ABOVE *A detail of 'Le Jeu de Boules'*
LEFT *Looking back down the enfilade. 'Le Jeu de Boules' is the second tapestry in the Gombaut and Macée set. The first four depict the lives of shepherds and shepherdesses at the ages of 10, 15, 20 and 25*

ABOVE *The blue damask armchair and stool in front of Raphael's dying Sapphira are thought to be from the Fourth State Room, the 'Blue Room'*

LEFT *Inspired by a 16th-century play, the mural of Cephalus and Aurora was painted to be viewed from the east entrance to the State Rooms. It may be by Giovanni Antonio Pellegrini, assisting Chéron, resembling his work at Kimbolton for a Montagu cousin*

OPPOSITE *The blanc-de-chine figurines are displayed in the State Rooms and the Great Hall (page 108) as they would have been in the 18th century, not in cabinets but on mantelpieces and open shelves. Clockwise from top left: a Guanyin (goddess of mercy) on a rockwork throne; an Immortal; standing Guanyins; mounted soldiers; and Buddhist monks*

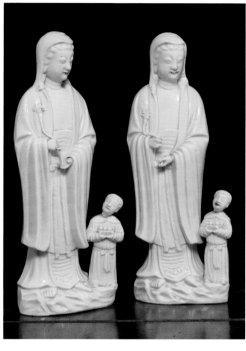

The Northwest Pavilion

One of the two wings jutting out from the North Front, this Pavilion was sumptuously embellished as the personal quarters of Ralph Montagu, combining English oak panelling with flamboyant French furniture

Jutting forward from the main block of the North Front are two wings, or Pavilions, with the same rusticated stonework and mansard roofs. Internally the Northeast Pavilion remains unfinished to this day. On the other hand, the Northwest Pavilion, once known as the 'White Pavilion', was crucial in making the house function.

We learn from early inventories that Ralph Montagu's own sleeping quarters were on the ground floor of this wing, known as the Low Pavilion. His bedroom, until recently the Duke's Study, was in the corner, and was preceded by a sitting or waiting room, the Anteroom, and followed by two small closets and a dressing room.

The same sequence, but altogether grander, with high ceilings and fine furnishings, can be found on the first floor, the High Pavilion. These rooms were intended for Ralph's second wife, the mad Dowager Duchess of Albemarle, who outlived Ralph, surviving until 1734. However, since she was confined to another

Montagu house, at Ditton, near London, or to her parents' London home, Newcastle House in Clerkenwell, the rooms were occupied by friends and relatives who sometimes settled in for weeks on end. Indeed, at the time of Ralph's death they are recorded as Lady Sandwich's Apartment, which, as the Countess of Sandwich was the wife of his first cousin, raises a few questions.

The dominant furniture in the Low and High Pavilions is French; most eye-catching is the metalwork marquetry. Ralph's taste for French furniture was to influence both the Montagus and the Buccleuchs, as reflected in additions made as late as the mid-19th century by the 5th and 6th Dukes of Buccleuch.

The oak-panelled walls throughout are hung with tapestries and portraits. The tapestries in the High Pavilion Bedroom – from the earlier of Boughton's two *Acts of the Apostles* sets, woven at Mortlake in the 1630s – are among the most magnificent in the house, with their scale, drama and vivid colour. Altogether more restful are the subtle greens and ochres of the Flemish tapestries of children in landscapes, woven a few decades later.

RIGHT *The exterior of the Northwest Pavilion. Both downstairs, in the Low Pavilion, and upstairs, in the High Pavilion, oak-panelled walls set off fashionable French furniture. The small-paned windows look French but are English sashes* LEFT *Ralph's Grand Etang seen from the attic of the Northwest Pavilion*

The Low Pavilion Anteroom

The Anteroom to Duke Ralph's apartment is now a gallery for remarkable religious paintings, mostly collected on their travels by the 3rd Duke and Duchess of Montagu and their son

For a hundred years now this has been the Anteroom to the Duke's office and that of his secretary, but in Ralph Montagu's time it was the entrance to a group of rooms intended for important visitors, and for Ralph himself, with the bedchamber and closet rooms beyond.

In the Anteroom the present Duke's father assembled a group of religious paintings reflecting the 18th-century tastes of the Cardigans, the future 3rd Duke of Montagu and his wife, and their son, John Brudenell, Marquess of Monthermer. Acquired in London and during their travels in France and Italy, they range from Madonnas by Italian Renaissance masters to *The Infant St John in the Wilderness* by Murillo. The rich inlaid furniture was certainly Ralph's: one of

ABOVE BENVENUTO TISI, CALLED IL GAROFALO (C.1481–1559)
The Holy Family with St Catherine
Monthermer bought this intimate late-Renaissance Ferrarese work from the dealer Thomas Jenkins in Rome in 1758. It is a small masterpiece, with its sensitive composition and atmospheric landscape
LEFT *One of four late-16th- or early-17th-century lightly gilded alabaster reliefs from Mechelen (Malines), near Antwerp, in its original frame*
RIGHT *'The Migration of Jacob' by Francesco Bassano the Younger (1549–92) hangs above the fireplace. The brass firedogs are contemporary with the Northwest Pavilion's beautifully carved oak bolection panelling. The rare Philippe Arbonnet (Arbuthnot) glass sconces were purchased in 1712*

the pair of mirrors and tables probably created for him by Gerrit Jensen, c.1690, includes his interlaced initials, RM, and the earl's coronet, which he acquired as Earl of Montagu in 1689. We also find a quite different style of furniture by Jensen: a table and matching pier glass japanned and veneered with incised Bantam lacquer. A monogram with the ducal coronet was added later.

One of the most historically important pieces in the house is an exotic writing table bearing the royal fleur-de-lys, c.1672, the work of Pierre Gole (c.1620–84). Seen here below Boughton's Murillo, this small desk, with its use of pewter and brass, almost certainly acquired by Ralph himself, represents a fashion that would reach its peak with the master craftsman André-Charles Boulle (1642–1732), who supplied much of the furniture in his eponymous style to Louis XIV between 1680 and 1715. Now identified as one of a pair made for Louis XIV, the desk is traditionally thought to have been a gift from the King to Ralph during his tenure as Ambassador to Versailles.

By contrast, the glass candle sconces either side of the fireplace (page 79), the work of Philippe Arbonnet (Arbuthnot), have a striking simplicity and purity of line. They were supplied by the Pelletier family, gifted Huguenot émigrés who were often employed by Ralph Montagu. Their survival after three centuries with their original brass fixings – in this room, in the Duke's Study next door and in the High Pavilion Bedroom – is extraordinary.

OPPOSITE *The Low Pavilion Anteroom, looking through to the Staircase Hall. Michael Dahl's oval portrait of Ralph Montagu is on the left. To the right of the door is a garlanded Madonna and Child, by Mario Nuzzi (Mario de' Fiori, 1603–73) and Sébastien Bourdon (1616–71). Next to it is Murillo's 'Infant St John in the Wilderness', c.1670. The top of the table in the centre is a piece of recycled wood marquetry with the monogram 'M', possibly once a decorative floor panel at Montagu House*

RIGHT *'The Rest on the Flight into Egypt' by Francesco Granacci (1477–1543) hangs above a chair with a tapestry cover by Huguenot weavers; three are named in the Montagu accounts as Marie Pariselle, Esther Régnaux and Madame Justell*

BELOW *This exquisite desk (c.1672), one of the house's highlights, is by Pierre Gole, 'ébéniste du roi' and Boulle's precursor. Its surface is crushed mother-of-pearl and pewter-on-brass marquetry*

The Duke's Study

The Low Pavilion Anteroom leads to what was once Ralph's bedchamber, which for the past century has served as the Duke's office

This room's eclectic plethora of desks is a reminder that, once Duke Ralph's bedroom, it has most recently been used as the Duke's Study, which connects to the office reserved for his secretary and two curious small rooms used for filing and miscellaneous storage. This office is now a reference library for the use of scholars researching the extensive archives.

Ralph was a keen patron of weavers, and tapestries were an integral part of the great house in 1700. Flemish panels have long been a feature of this room; indeed, tapestry has been the only wall covering ever used, as evidenced by the basic bare plaster behind it.

RIGHT *These Flemish tapestries of children by a waterfall, c.1660–75, were lengthened by the Huguenot weaver John Vanderbank for Ralph's 'Bedchamber and Dressing Room'. He wove two new ones to match in 1704 at a cost of £48. Above the fireplace is Ralph's first father-in-law, Thomas Wriothesley, 4th Earl of Southampton*

BELOW LEFT *A photograph of the present Duke's grandmother, Mollie, 8th Duchess of Buccleuch, beside that of the wedding of her sister-in-law Lady Alice Montagu Douglas Scott to Prince Henry, Duke of Gloucester, in 1935. Next to the portrait of a lady by Mary Beale (1633–99) is a George III stick barometer by Ramsden of London*
BELOW *A detail of the tapestry, right*

The High Pavilion Anteroom

This entrance to the upper floor of the Northwest Pavilion is a gallery for some of Boughton's most striking portraits and exuberant French furniture

The portraits in the High Pavilion Anteroom tend to have a family connection – if not to the direct line, then to aunts, uncles and remoter cousins. The most notable exceptions are the striking pair of a surgeon and his wife by Pieter Pourbus, and the proud portrait in shining armour of Sir Thomas Tresham, the ardently Roman Catholic neighbour who built the nearby Lyveden New Bield and the Triangular Lodge at Rushton, both of which in their decorative features were risky demonstrations of his forbidden faith.

Behind the door, as you enter from the Staircase Hall, the armoured portrait of dashing Edward (Ned) Montagu hangs as a reminder that Ralph Montagu had an elder brother (page 17). After Cromwell's death, Ned acted as a go-between for his powerful cousin and namesake Edward Montagu, who commanded the Commonwealth's navy, and the exiled Charles II. After the Restoration he gained the position of Master of the Queen's Horse. But he made the serious error of being too forward with the Queen, Catherine of Braganza. He was dismissed and his post went to Ralph.

The room contains examples of important French furniture. The Colbert Cabinet, c.1700, bears the coat of arms of Jean-Baptiste-Michel Colbert, Archbishop of Toulouse. He was the son of Louis XIV's all-powerful Minister of Finances, who had introduced the cabinetmaker André-Charles Boulle to the King. It was purchased by the 3rd Duke and

LEFT *The Colbert Cabinet, c.1700, Boughton's most flamboyant piece of furniture by Boulle, stands beneath the 1st Lord Montagu in red peer's robes (far left). On either side are pedestal cabinets by Étienne Levasseur, 1775–80. Duke Ralph liked assembling pictures of prominent men in recent history. In the centre of the right-hand wall is the Emperor Charles V, above a portrait of the Bohemian engraver Wenceslaus Hollar. A posthumous portrait of Ralph's brother, Ned, who was killed in action in 1665, is to the right of the door*

ABOVE *One of the gilt-bronze mounts on the Colbert Cabinet*

his Duchess at the Duc de Tallard's sale in Paris in 1756. The later pair of pedestal cabinets on either side are by Étienne Levasseur (1721–98). These are dated to 1775–80 and show the more architectural Neoclassical style in which Boulle marquetry was revived during the Louis XVI period.

The Levasseur cabinets were acquired by the 5th Duke of Buccleuch in 1830, and reflect both the enduring family interest in French furniture and the general popularity of Louis XV and Louis XVI furniture in England from the 1830s onwards.

ABOVE *A flower painting by Jean-Baptiste Monnoyer (1636–99) hangs above the fireplace. The rare English crystal chandelier is contemporary*

LEFT MICHAEL VAN MIEREVELT (1567–1641) **Sir Ralph Winwood of Ditton (c.1563–1617)** *Duke Ralph's grandfather was Ambassador to the Dutch Republic and Secretary of State under James I. His papers at Boughton are an important historical resource. Winwood encouraged Sir Walter Raleigh to attack the Spanish in 1617, which led to Raleigh's execution; he died before he could suffer the same fate. Lady Winwood helped to raise Duke Ralph, who was named after him but never knew him*

Sir Thomas Tresham of Rushton (1543–1605)

A Tudor politician and ardent Roman Catholic, Tresham's convictions are evident in the nearby Triangular Lodge – a play on the symbolism of the Trinity, and a dangerous sign of his faith. The trefoils on his armour are also symbolic and an allusion to his surname. Tresham was among the Northamptonshire landowners implicated in the Gunpowder Plot, and his son died in the Tower for his own part in it

BELOW ENGLISH SCHOOL, C.1610

Edward, 1st Lord Montagu of Boughton (1562–1644)

To distance himself from the plotters and to reassure a suspicious James I, the 1st Lord Montagu tabled a motion in Parliament to turn November 5 into a day of thanksgiving for the failure of the plot, today's Guy Fawkes Day. Privately, though, he still helped the widowed Lady Tresham, his neighbour; her letter of thanks remains in the archives. Later distressed by the division between King and Parliament, he sent horses and weapons to the King. Parliament put him in the Tower, and he died still under house arrest

The High Pavilion Bedroom

Once enjoying a sensational view, this room is now almost always shuttered to protect its unexpectedly vivid 17th-century tapestries

This large corner room, intended for Duke Ralph's second wife, the Dowager Duchess of Albemarle, is dominated by two exceptionally well-preserved, vividly coloured pieces from the Mortlake tapestry factory. The tapestries were woven during the reign of Charles I, who had purchased the cartoons by Raphael from which they were made. They represent *Christ's Charge to Peter* and *Elymas the Sorcerer Struck by Blindness*, and are part of a set of eight panels woven in 1638–40, each bearing the weaver's monogram. The four at Boughton, together with *The Miraculous Draught of Fishes*, on loan to the Victoria and Albert Museum, were probably bought by Ralph's father, the 2nd Lord Montagu, at the late Earl of Pembroke's sale in 1649 – they have the Pembroke arms at the top. The other three were bought by Cardinal Mazarin and survive in the Palazzo Ducale in Urbino.

Tapestry is especially vulnerable to damage by light, which fades the colours and weakens the threads. For this reason, the shutters here are rarely opened – sadly excluding the views to the north over the newly restored Grand Etang and down the Lime Avenue, which this pivotal room was intended to enjoy.

Concealed behind the tapestries, where they meet, are discreet doors to the bathroom and a clothes closet. On the bed is one of the Mortlake sumpter cloths that covered the pack animals in Ralph's baggage train as he entered Paris as Charles II's Ambassador.

LEFT *The tapestries 'Christ's Charge to Peter' (left) and 'Elymas the Sorcerer Struck by Blindness' were woven from Raphael cartoons in 1638–40. Below the blind Elymas is a rosewood commode, c.1760, by Pierre Langlois, an 'ébéniste' with a workshop in Tottenham Court Road. Very tall doors, concealed by the tapestries, lead to a bathroom and clothes closet*

TOP *Above the bed in the dressing room, with its Jacobean needlework bedhead and coverlet, is the Marquis de Louvois (1641–91), Louis XIV's minister of war, by Sébastien Bourdon*

ABOVE *The handsome Victorian water closet in the bathroom of the High Pavilion Bedroom, which is hung with Antwerp tapestries from the Marcus Aurelius set, c.1660–70*

Duke Ralph's Unfinished Wing

One great surprise at Boughton, and a rare architectural curiosity, is the incomplete Northeast Pavilion

The orderly appearance of the north façade gives no inkling of the great void within its Northeast Pavilion, also known as the Unfinished Wing. With the exception of attic rooms, whose floors rest high above, it is a shell with two cavernous spaces, bare of plaster, criss-crossed by massive oak beams that should have supported the grandest of apartments. At the first-floor level, a door destined never to be used leads back into the State Rooms. Within living memory there was nothing here but a dusty earthen floor and an ancient ladder or two.

One day archival research may provide a concrete trail of explanation, but it is not difficult to imagine the pressures of finance and time faced by Duke Ralph, given the scale of his ambitious building projects. For his son John, with his interest in refashioning the landscape and his own pet building project, the new Montagu House in Whitehall, completion of his father's vision must have been a low priority.

One silver lining for us today is the architectural insight provided by the exposure of late-17th-century construction methods and building materials. Oak trees

ABOVE *Lively dragons seen against a golden sky inside the Chinese Pavilion (pictured opposite), built as a 'tea pavilion' in 1745 for Duke John's riverside terrace at Montagu House, Whitehall. Easily dismantled, the oilcloth panels slot together*

LEFT *Sunlight pours through the windows of the Unfinished Wing, perfect on the outside, but a shell internally. After his father's death, Duke John completed the attic for use as servants' bedrooms. He also had plans drawn up for the main floors*

OPPOSITE *With its exposed oak beams and hidden downpipes, the Unfinished Wing is now home to the Chinese Pavilion, sturdy braziers and sculpted busts from the Colonnade. For a time the archives were stored here in wooden bunkers*

hundreds of years old would have been needed to furnish the giant beams that run at odd angles across the void. The incorporation of the rainwater downpipes within the fabric of the walls, which one only notices from inside, cleverly reduces an element of clutter from the harmony of the façade.

Perhaps inevitably, such valuable covered space has come to be filled with a truly eclectic mix – busts and other statuary brought indoors for safekeeping, braziers, travelling trunks that were perhaps used by Duke Ralph on ambassadorial duties, as well as the magnificent garden benches from the Colonnade by George Nix and one of the earliest billiard tables in England.

Adding to the sense of surprise in this Aladdin's cave is the 'Chinese Pavilion' ordered by the 2nd Duke from 'Samuel Smith Tentmaker' and paid for on November 29, 1745. This summerhouse, made of timber and oilcloth, was originally placed on the terrace overlooking the Thames at the new Montagu House, in Whitehall, where it appears in a contemporary riverscape painting by Canaletto. It could be dismantled easily for winter storage, the dragon on the apex being a linchpin, and remained in regular use until the 1960s, when it was erected each year on the west lawn at Boughton. It has recently been joined by an enormous 17th-century Chinese screen, which used to stand at the end of the Great Hall and has been in storage for 50 years.

ABOVE *The antiquarian William Stukeley advised the 2nd Duke to convert the Unfinished Wing into a Gothic chapel – a project, like the park bridge, that Duke John resisted*

LEFT *A coromandel lacquer screen from the first half of the reign of the Emperor Kangxi (1661–1722). The archives show a payment of £10 to the Huguenot Charles Motteux in 1711. The family had links to the East India Company dating back as early as the first expedition to Japan in 1611*

FAR LEFT *Fittingly, the 12-fold Chinese screen – 8 metres in width – is next to Duke John's Chinese Pavilion, whose panels open to reveal the old buttoned seating and woven-mat flooring*

ABOVE *The garden benches by George Nix have been brought in from the Colonnade outside*

RIGHT *The full-size oak billiard table is one of the earliest built in England. One of three supplied to the 1st Duke by the Huguenot craftsman Pierre Rieusset, it was delivered in 1695 and installed in an attic to provide entertainment for the servants*

THE TUDOR MANOR

The heart of the house

At the centre of everything, hidden by the unexpected French North Front and the formal State Rooms, lies another surprise: a very English country house that grew up round a maze of 16th-century courtyards

Behind its imposing north façade Boughton conceals a much less regimented cluster of building elevations, chimney stacks and courtyards. The Fish Court, the largest of the courtyards, sits at the core of the 16th-century house, and from here the true outline and steeply pitched roof of the Great Hall is apparent. Attached to this hall, to the left, lies the Little Hall, once, on its upper storey, part of the Great Chamber on the first floor. To the right is the Egyptian Hall. Each of these spaces was radically transformed by Duke Ralph, for the most part internally, but also by the introduction of much larger, longer windows. The small Tudor windows of the Library, once part of the Great Chamber, are the only traces of what went before.

From the Fish Court it is possible to guess at the slow evolution of the building during the later 16th and earlier 17th century: how it was first made into an open courtyard with the South Side, which at one time contained a chapel, and how it was enclosed in the 1570s by extending the West Front.

It is far from clear how the courtyard's eastern side, now occupied by the Audit Room,

A COURTYARD MANOR HOUSE
Boughton developed round a series of courtyards between the 16th and 18th centuries, becoming a labyrinth of rooms and corridors full of light and garden scents. The Great Hall of the orginal Tudor manor house was entered from the Fish Court (right of photograph); the Clock Court (on the left) has always been the hub of the working house. In the background, beyond the screen of chimneys, are the Rose Garden and the Lily Pond

evolved; it was not until the 2nd Duke's time, in the late 1740s, that the Fish Court reached its final incarnation. Final with one important exception: at some point the small pond was removed and until the 1970s a plinth and urn stood at its heart, around which guests at house parties draped themselves.

The present Duke's parents decided the courtyard should justify its name, reintroducing a pond and fountain. They also added the surrounding borders. The late Duchess Jane was responsible for the planting, which is as nearly pure white as respect for some ancient roses allows.

OPPOSITE *The Great Hall, with its 16th-century finials and gables. This was the entrance in Tudor times, with parlours and chambers on the left, and service rooms on the right. The upstairs Library (in the left corner), once part of the Great Chamber, has kept the only Tudor windows left in the house*

ABOVE *The view across the Fish Court to the South Side, once a separate building with a Tudor chapel. This was joined to the manor house by the addition of the wing containing the Long Gallery (on the right) in 1579–80 and turned into living quarters in 1741–43. The low Audit Room (on the left) was built as a music gallery in 1746–47*

LEFT *The Great Hall in 1938. House guests would have tea in the Fish Court and congregate round the urn at its centre. The pond and fountain were reintroduced in the 1970s*

The Great Hall

The original Tudor hall was retained, but Duke Ralph transformed it with a new barrel-vaulted ceiling and greatly enlarged windows

The Great Hall, the largest single space at Boughton, serves many purposes today, as occasional dining room and even more occasional concert hall, with the barrel ceiling making for wonderful acoustics. A *Country Life* photograph from early in the last century shows it with bare brick and plaster (page 39) before the oak panelling, the work of the estate's own craftsmen, was installed in 1911. One Tudor doorway with stone surrounds was left revealed, to act as a display arch for blanc-de-chine porcelain; two others are concealed underneath the panelling.

Also anchoring us in the 16th century are portraits not just of the early Montagus but of Elizabeth I and her one-time favourite, the 3rd Earl of Southampton, Shakespeare's great friend. Southampton and his wife, Elizabeth Vernon, whose portrait hangs beside him, were, in today's jargon, one of the power couples of their time, whose influence was considerable, not least in the field of fashion. Their granddaughter and heiress, also Elizabeth, was to be the first of Duke Ralph's wives and the mother of the 2nd Duke.

It is hard to imagine the room without *The Elements* – its great late-17th-century tapestry series, each with its Montagu coat of arms and the RM monogram – and hard not to have the eye caught by the massive plaster coat of arms that leans out high above the hall (overleaf). In 1705 the carver Gideon du Chesne noted that

he 'took down an Earls coronet in the Great Hall and made in the room a Dukes coronet'.

Yet such obvious pride in family is given a degree of pathos by the dominating presence above the fireplace of the ill-fated James, Duke of Monmouth and 1st Duke of Buccleuch, on horseback. His Buccleuch descendants were to subsume, through marriage, this line of Montagus and their lands. Elizabeth Montagu, the crucial link in that chain, sensitively portrayed by Gainsborough, is to the left of the doorway to the Little Hall. On an easel nearby is Pompeo Batoni's portrait of her brother, Lord Monthermer, whose early death extinguished the last hope for the Montagu dukedom.

Statues of two French kings on horseback, Louis IX (St Louis) in parcel-gilt and Louis XIV in bronze, take their places either side of the fireplace and remind us again of Boughton's French influences, most visibly exemplified by the two marriage coffers by Boulle either side of the doorway opposite them.

For a room of this scale, the Great Hall remains surprisingly warm in all seasons, helped by the south-facing aspect of its long windows and by a huge fireplace for a log fire, which delivers both an intense heat that permeates the whole space and the familiar waft of woodsmoke.

OPPOSITE THE GREAT HALL, LOOKING EAST
In 1695 the inconspicuous door at the end of the fireplace wall was where William III entered the house from the North Front. Chéron's mural of the 'Apotheosis of Hercules' was ordered in 1706 to celebrate the acquisition of the dukedom and the marriage of the future Duke John. Ralph's four 'Elements' tapestries ('Air' is on the left, 'Earth' above the door) were hung here in 1911. The walls were originally panelled from floor to ceiling, with an upper tier of portraits and, over the fire, a plaster relief of 'Hercules Rescuing Alcestis from the Underworld'. The equestrian portrait replacing it would have pleased Ralph, an admirer of its subject: Charles II's tragic son, the Duke of Monmouth

BELOW *The Gothic revivalist Sir Arthur Blomfield (1829–99) proposed removing the Great Hall's painted vault to reveal the Tudor beamed ceiling*

OVERLEAF THE GREAT HALL, LOOKING WEST
Hanging beneath the tapestry 'Fire' are the 3rd Duke of Montagu, by Sir William Beechey; his wife, Mary, and daughter Elizabeth, Duchess of Buccleuch, by Gainsborough; and, on the easel, Lord Monthermer, their son, by Batoni. To the left of the fireplace is a statue of Louis XIV, and to the right one of Louis IX

THE MONARCH
IN THE GREAT HALL

LEFT FOLLOWER OF MARCUS
GHEERAERTS THE YOUNGER
(C.1561–1636)
Queen Elizabeth I
(R.1558–1603)
*This portrait of the Queen is
unusual in showing her age.
The inscription places her in the
'thirty-seventh year of her
reign, 1595', when she was in
her early sixties. An intriguing
twin version is in the home of
the Dean of Westminster*

OPPOSITE
ATTRIBUTED TO MARCUS
GHEERAERTS THE YOUNGER
Portrait of a Lady
*This portrait is traditionally
believed to be Elizabeth Jeffrey,
first wife of the 1st Lord
Montagu. The fashion for
Elizabethan dresses was
revived by James I's Queen,
Anne of Denmark, in the 1610s,
perhaps from a wish to
recapture past glory. But, as the
costume historian Judith
Hodgkinson suggests, the cut of
the richly ornamented sleeves,
wide at the top and tapering,
the square neckline and the
astonishing gold chain date the
portrait to the Elizabethan age,
c.1600, which means that it may
well be of Elizabeth Jeffrey, or
even her mother-in-law
Elizabeth Harington*

SHAKESPEARE'S PATRONS
IN THE GREAT HALL
*These portraits of the Earl and
Countess of Southampton came
into the family when Ralph Montagu
married their granddaughter
Elizabeth Wriothesley in 1673*

OPPOSITE ATTRIBUTED TO JOHN
DE CRITZ THE ELDER
(1551/2–1642)
**Henry Wriothesley, 3rd Earl of
Southampton (1573–1624)**
*The imprisonment of Shakespeare's
great patron in the Tower of London for
his part in the Earl of Essex's uprising
of 1601 is commemorated in this
portrait. The Tower is seen in the top
right corner with the dates of his
incarceration, February 1600 to April
1603, and the words 'Unconquered
though in chains'. The cat, the Earl's
favourite, supposedly found its way into
the Tower by climbing down a chimney*

RIGHT ENGLISH SCHOOL, c.1600
**Elizabeth Vernon, Countess of
Southampton (c.1572–1655)**
*One of two highly intimate portraits of
the wife of the 3rd Earl, a Maid of
Honour to the Queen (see page 117).
Here she is seen dressing, in a floral
bedgown and pearls, as if looking into
a mirror – her lace collar hangs on the
curtain. On the dressing table are more
jewels and a large pincushion*

EXUBERANT FIGURES IN THE TUDOR HALL
ABOVE LEFT *The rococo wine cup in the centre is by Charles Frederick Kandler, 1749. The chased jars either side are by Queen Anne's goldsmith Anthony Nelme. To match the Kandler cup, in 1829 Robert Garrard added putti to the lids and figures as handles*
ABOVE CENTRE *An arched doorway, the only Tudor feature still visible, serves as a niche for blanc-de-chine figurines. Next to it are Lord Monthermer, by Batoni, and his sister Elizabeth, by Gainsborough*
ABOVE RIGHT *A bracket clock by Gloria of Rouen, in a Boulle case made in Paris, 1725–30. Lively ormolu figures include a musician and a dragon*
LEFT *Sea horses draw Neptune's chariot in the tapestry 'Water', part of the 'Elements' series. His companion Amphitrite bears a shield to which Ralph's monogram and Earl's coronet had been added by 1695, as they were to 'Earth' and 'Air'*
OPPOSITE AND RIGHT *'The Apotheosis of Hercules' (1706–07), Chéron's Boughton finale. A bricklayer at Ditton, the Duke's house in Buckinghamshire, where Chéron also worked, was paid to model as Hercules*

The Egyptian Hall

While the Great Hall was certainly used for large gatherings, the room known as the 'Egyptian Hall' is regularly described in documents from the early 1700s as the Dining Room

The Egyptian Hall was used more regularly as a dining room by Dukes Ralph and John than the adjacent Great Hall. John belonged to the newly founded Egyptian Society, whose members were accustomed to dining in each other's houses, which presumably gave rise to the hall's name. No doubt evocative of the spirited gatherings in the room, Chéron's ceiling portrays a rotund Bacchus riding an ass with accompanying putti and bacchanalian accoutrements.

A fellow member and friend of Duke John's, the antiquarian Dr William Stukeley, a pioneer of archaeology at Stonehenge, received much patronage from the Duke and in return was constantly proffering advice. He had ideas about how the park might be improved, including a flowery, Gothic-style bridge to replace the original simple classical structure that remains to this day. Thankfully, it went no further than the construction of the wooden model in this room.

Portraits line the walls, with many of the subjects portrayed in black. It is said that some were overpainted to show that they were in mourning. However, it is a purchase of the 3rd Duke and his wife, Mary, in Paris that takes pride of place above the fireplace. *The Adoration of the Shepherds* is now known to be an early work by El Greco, though when it was bought it was believed to be by Tintoretto, then more highly esteemed.

THE DUKE'S DINING ROOM
The Egyptian Hall, hung with mainly family portraits, is bathed in light from the Clock Court. The table on the right supports William Stukeley's model for a Gothic bridge in the park, made by the capable clockmaker and bell-founder Thomas Eayre of Kettering. El Greco's 'Adoration of the Shepherds' hangs above the fireplace. Two Georgian mahogany spinning wheels are displayed on the 17th-century scrubbed-oak refectory table

RIGHT DOMENIKOS THEOTOKOPOULOS, CALLED EL GRECO (1541–1614)
The Adoration of the Shepherds, c.1574–75
This altarpiece, with its shadowy atmosphere and attenuated figures, is now known to be an early work by El Greco, before his arrival at the Spanish court. It was bought for £27 by the 3rd Duke and his wife in Paris at the Duc de Tallard's sale in March 1756. The dramatic plunge into depth created by the entourage of the Magi in the background shows El Greco's Mannerist leanings

LEFT *These late-16th- and early-17th-century paintings, with their lace ruffs and ropes of pearls, are mostly family portraits. They show Elizabeth Jeffrey (bottom left), the 1st Lord Montagu's wife, who died in 1611. His second wife, the 'much talker' Frances Cotton, appears behind Stukeley's bridge, flanked by the 3rd Earl of Southampton and his Countess, the grandparents of Duke Ralph's first wife*

Lucy Russell (née Harington), Countess of Bedford (1580–1627)
The niece of the 2nd Sir Edward Montagu's wife is portrayed in fashionable needlelace collar fingering the ornate case of a portrait miniature. Her brother was the erudite courtier Sir John Harington, who invented the flushing toilet. An intriguing figure, famous for her patronage of Jacobean poets and musicians, Lucy was praised by Ben Jonson for her 'manly soul'. John Donne addressed poems to her and she was godmother to his second daughter. The work of Michael Drayton, another poet who benefited from her patronage, survives in the archives at Bowhill. Described as a Calvinist, she nevertheless staged masques at court and even performed in them bare-breasted

Top left English School, 17th century
James Montagu, Bishop of Bath and Wells and Bishop of Winchester (1568–1618)
One of the 1st Lord Montagu's five brothers, James became the first Master of Sidney Sussex College, Cambridge, in 1599, aged 28, forging a family link maintained to this day. Close to James I, he assisted with the drafting of the King James Bible and later, as Bishop of Bath and Wells, with the restoration of Bath Abbey – the Great West Doors bear the Montagu arms in his memory

Top right Circle of John Parker, 17th century
This unidentified sitter holds a pink rose and is extravagantly bedecked in ribbons and pearls

Bottom Left Circle of Cornelius Jonson
Elizabeth Montagu, Countess of Lindsey (1586–1654)
The 1st Lord Montagu's daughter lost her husband, a Royalist, at Edgehill (1642). 'I never will fight in the same field with boys again' were his last words

Bottom right
After Robert Walker
Oliver Cromwell (1599–1658)
The Pelletiers' 1709 bill for 'mending' the Lord Protector's portrait (page 109) shows, surprisingly, that it was in the house in Duke Ralph's day

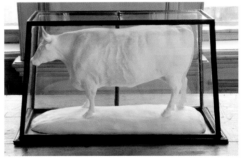

Top *Bacchus riding high in the Egyptian Hall.*
After a visit in 1763, the writer and antiquarian
Horace Walpole commented that 'gods and goddesses
lived over my head in every room'
Above *A Teeswater Shorthorn cow from the*
Buccleuch herd, by George Garrard (1760–1826)
Right *At the end of the room hangs a full-length*
portrait of a forebear of the 3rd Duke of Montagu:
the duplicitous politician Thomas Savile, Earl of
Sussex (1591–1656), painted in peer's robes by
George Geldorp (1595–1665). The stone flooring
still bears the rust marks left by the metal racking
used by the British Museum to store their artefacts
for safekeeping during the Second World War

Elizabeth
Countesse
ampton;

Vernon,
of Soutl

RIGHT ENGLISH SCHOOL,
17TH CENTURY

**Elizabeth Vernon,
Countess of Southampton,
c.1600**

*The décolleté flowered dress
and pearl-trimmed coat come
as a surprising contrast to the
black costumes of the other
portraits in the Egyptian Hall.
In 1598, Elizabeth Vernon
discovered that she was
pregnant while her lover, the
3rd Earl of Southampton, was
in France on a diplomatic
mission for Queen Elizabeth.
He slipped back secretly to
marry her before returning to
France. Furious when she
found out, the Queen had both
of them thrown into Fleet
Prison. Their granddaughter
Elizabeth Wriothesley
married Ralph Montagu.
The 2nd Duke would inherit
this painting from her, along
with her portrait in the Great
Hall (page 106). Another
legacy was the Abbey of
Beaulieu, near Southampton*

The Little Hall

Two Tudor rooms were transformed by Duke Ralph into an atmospheric double-height space, with an impressive gallery and painted ceiling. Despite its modest name, this served for a long time as the crossroads of the house

As in the adjoining Great Hall, the Little Hall's massive fireplace is a great provider of warmth; it also features a stone-carved family tree. Duke Ralph opened the space up to the full height of the building and created an elevated passageway akin to a minstrels' gallery along the west side. The result, slightly disconcertingly, is space for an upper tier of full-length portraits, which include Duke John in his Garter robes and his wife, Mary Churchill (opposite), in orange silks with an Indian palanquin. The portrait by Anton Raphael Mengs of the 3rd Duke's son, Lord Monthermer, swathed in fur and accompanied by a large hound (page 125), makes a distinct contrast with his portrait by Batoni (page 200).

Once again, the Montagus find themselves cheek by jowl with the Buccleuch side of the family in this room: Monmouth, again, and his wife, Anna Scott (both above the fireplace), his father, Charles II (page 125), and, jumping back two generations, his maternal great-grandfather Henri IV of France – both as a bust above the fireplace, by Hubert Le Sueur, and painted on a white charger (page 120).

Just as eye-catching are the paintings collected by Monthermer and his parents. The *Young Man in a Plumed Hat* by Annibale Carracci to the right of the fireplace may have been brought back from Monthermer's travels in Italy. His parents bought the large landscape by David Teniers the Younger (page 122). At £74, it was the most expensive painting they ever acquired.

OPPOSITE *The stone overmantel in the Little Hall traces Ralph Montagu's ancestors back to Drogo de Monte Acuto, the Norman ancestor of the medieval Montecutes (Montagus), on the left, and William the Conqueror on the right. The 2nd Duke appears in the hunting scene by John Wootton above the sofa. Above the Wootton is a full-length portrait of his wife, Mary Churchill. A bust of Henri IV of France, by Hubert Le Sueur, stands between two gilded eagles from Adderbury, a Buccleuch seat in Oxfordshire*

LEFT *'Young Man in a Plumed Hat', by Annibale Carracci, c.1585. The collar and feathers allow the Bolognese artist to show off his handling of light in the Venetian manner. Below it is a 1944 head of the 9th Duke by Oscar Nemon, best known for his statue of Churchill*

LEFT *Chéron's mural 'The Return of Proserpine' is best viewed from the gallery, built in 1694 when Duke Ralph created the double-height space. Before this, the upper half of the Little Hall and the Library, with its vaulted ceiling (near left), formed the Tudor Great Chamber. The ceiling was painted c.1707, at the same time as the mural in the Great Hall, Chéron's last commission at Boughton. The subject is taken from Ovid's 'Metamorphosis'. After her abduction to the Underworld by Pluto, Proserpine is allowed to return to Earth each spring*

Next to the door to the Lbrary is a portrait of Lord Monthermer with a bust of Cicero, painted in Rome in 1758 by Anton Raphael Mengs (1728–79). To his left is Charles II, by the studio of Sir Peter Lely, c.1680, and next to the King is the 2nd Duke, by Charles Jervas. Both are wearing Garter robes

THE WEST FRONT

Duke John's legacy

The 2nd Duke's enquiring spirit lives on in an orderly façade that conceals a palimpsest – rooms with layers of Tudor refinement, Baroque grandeur and 20th-century informality

The coherent block that the West Front appears to be when seen across the lawn, with its neat roof-level balustrading, is anything but when explored inside. Contrasted within it are the two-storey grandeur of the Staircase Hall and the Little Hall at one end and, at the other, the intimacy of one of the smallest rooms in the house, the Boudoir, with a complete cross section of living and sleeping spaces in between.

Few of these rooms, with the distinguished exception of the Library, have retained their primary purposes over the years since Duke John's time. Indeed, many have been chopped and changed as walls have been moved and doorways opened up or closed. The Nursery

RIGHT *Weldon stone ties together the two architectural styles of Duke Ralph's mansarded North Front and Staircase Hall (on the left) and Duke John's West Front (on the right). French windows in both allow you to step straight into the landscape. Only a few lead urns survive from the formal gardens – most, along with countless statues, had been sold off by 1796*

Stairs didn't exist until a century ago. Three generations back, today's Rainbow Room was the family dining room. Photography reinforces the point. For instance, note the dramatic change made in the Drawing Room by the large, architectural stone fireplace (brought from another Montagu house in Northamptonshire in 1910), and see how John Fowler's elegance contrasts with the Victorian clutter of a century earlier (page 147).

Along with structural and decorative alterations, patterns of occupation have changed with the generations. Until recently the Little Hall was a principal living space, the crossroads of the house, where family and guests traditionally gathered. Now the Morning Room has assumed that role, and that is itself being overtaken by fresh enthusiasm for using the adjoining Loggia, with its glazed arches and doors to the West Lawn, providing a sunny, conservatory-like sitting area.

ABOVE *The Loggia, with its 17th-century Italian marble font, sunloungers and croquet mallets* LEFT AND TOP LEFT *The view to the Broad Water. The lawn ends halfway down the avenue in a ha-ha. Boughton had some two miles of ha-has, most now hidden by centuries of leaf mould*

The Loggia

Although they seem to fit naturally with the façade, the glazed French windows were installed only a century ago, undoing the work of the 2nd Duke, who had created an Italian-style loggia with open arches (page 37). Until recently a storage place for cricketing and croquet equipment and decorous sunloungers for the lawns, it has been tidied up to provide a natural sitting area for house guests and occasional events.

Not only does it give directly onto the Morning Room, the most comfortable sitting room, but a door at the opposite end leads to the Boudoir, the South Passage and the Nursery Stairs, which give easy access to all other areas of the house.

The Boudoir

Discreet and calm, this jewel of a room, with its perfect proportions and beautiful wall panels, was the late Duchess's sitting room

I solated in the southwest corner of the building is one of the most perfectly proportioned and appealing of the rooms at Boughton. The Boudoir, with its view of the Broad Water, has for generations been the Duchess's sitting room, as it was for the late Duchess Jane. Its subtle pale-blue walls are an ideal background for the wall panels by the influential Huguenot designer Daniel Marot, some of the most significant items in the house. Painted on canvas, they were once part of a larger set

LEFT SIR GODFREY KNELLER (1646–1723)
Marquess of Blandford, aged 16
The heir apparent to the Duke of Marlborough died of smallpox in 1703, a year after this portrait was painted. The English frame is c.1735
RIGHT DANIEL MAROT (1661–1752)
Wall panels with scenes of Apollo and Daphne
Part of a set of panels that once lined the walls of a room in Montagu House in Bloomsbury
OPPOSITE *Above the fireplace is the 2nd Duke, by George Knapton. The 18th-century fire screen has a Beauvais tapestry depicting a silver pheasant*

that decorated the walls of an entire room, covering it with mythological scenes such as the transformation of Daphne into a tree, with delightful detailing in the floral garlands and arabesques.

The Boudoir provides an appropriate home for smaller pictures such as a 17th-century French miniature of a young man in black with a white collar (left of fireplace) and portraits of the 2nd Duke and his wife's brother the Marquess of Blandford as boys. Both have striking oval giltwood frames.

The Boudoir Lobby

It seems odd in a building as large as Boughton to find spaces that are intimate, almost cramped. As such, the Lobby provides a perfect gallery for the small, predominantly Dutch paintings that were so popular with British collectors in the 17th and 18th centuries and were particular favourites of the 3rd Duke and Duchess. A mix of oils and gouaches, they are a tribute to the skills of conservators at the Hamilton Kerr Institute near Cambridge and the Paper Conservation Workshop at Duxford. Eight years ago, a burst pipe immersed them all in water. Clouding of the varnish made them frighteningly invisible, and the gesso of the frames became completely soggy. After several years' work they have been restored to pristine condition, with the exception of staining on two of the watercolours.

Note particularly the little Van der Heyden of a square, possibly in Cologne, and the two scenes of horsemen by Philips Wouwerman. Especially eye-catching for the strength of its colouring is a small landscape with bridge and fishermen by Paul Brill. The restoration process does, however, highlight an issue for country-house collections, which tend to be less frequently cleaned than paintings in museums and galleries, with the result that the yellowing varnish gives them a distinctive patina of age. Paintings beyond the Lobby in the South Passage, such as the small Ruysdael and the Ostade, reinforce the point.

LEFT *Looking down the South Passage from the Boudoir Lobby, hung with Dutch paintings bought by the 3rd Duke and Duchess, who toured the Low Countries in the 1750s, and gouaches by Johann Wilhelm Baur. The 17th-century Japanese lacquer coffer is painted with pagodas and rockwork*

PAUL BRILL (1554–1626)
A river scene with fishermen drawing nets from a high arched bridge

JAN VAN DER HEYDEN (1637–1712)
A street scene thought to be in Cologne

PHILIPS WOUWERMAN (1619–68)
Cavaliers exercising horses in a riding school

LEFT Gerard Houckgeest
(c.1600–60)
**The interior of the
Oude Kerk, Delft**

BOTTOM LEFT
JOHN WOOTTON (c.1682–1764)
A bay with a ruined temple, 1755

BELOW
GEORGE BARRET (c.1730–84)
Mares and foals in a field

OPPOSITE, TOP
FRANCIS SARTORIUS (1734–1804)
**A grey stallion presented to the
Duke of Montagu by George III**
*Halfway up the Nursery Staircase, a
groom in royal livery holds the horse
given to the 3rd Duke in 1785, when
he was Master of the Horse*

OPPOSITE, BELOW
JOHANN WILHELM BAUR
(1607–40)
**The Villa Borghese
and The Villa Aldobrandini**
*Fine gouaches in the
Boudoir Lobby*

The South Passage

The cool greys of the Boudoir Lobby permeate the length of the South Passage. Its stone flags are usually softened by a specially woven runner with the Montagu lozenges. Bordering the Fish Court, this passage is a wonderful vantage point for looking across to the Great Hall, particularly when it is lit up at night, creating a sense of life and festivity at the heart of the house.

An eclectic mix of paintings can be found here, Dutch and Italianate in particular, as well as Samuel Scott's view of the second Montagu House, in Whitehall, and a lively interior scene of a musical entertainment, possibly in the London house of the Cardigans, the future 3rd Duke and Duchess, captured in his cartoon style by Marcellus Laroon.

Strange though it will sound, Boughton is perennially short of hanging spaces, particularly tall and wide ones like those offered by the walls of the staircase leading up to the Nursery. Here, long panels by Louis Laguerre and large flower paintings by Monnoyer can rub shoulders with the wonderful grey stallion by Francis Sartorius, a gift from George III to the 3rd Duke.

Top right Marcellus Laroon the Younger (1679–1772)
A musical tea party
Probably a party given by the Cardigans. Laroon painted interiors for George I as well as two Dukes of Montagu, many showing musicians. Another Huguenot, he combined careers as a soldier, violinist and painter
Right Samuel Scott (1702–72)
The Thames from Westminster Bridge, with Montagu House
The house fronted directly onto the river, before the construction of the Embankment in the 1860s
Opposite *The beautifully simple South Passage*

The Rainbow Room

The overmantel in the Rainbow Room harks back to the Tudor origins of this part of the house, contrasting with French royal portraits and an elegant Boulle writing table, among the finest of its kind

In the late 19th and early 20th century, this was a dining room. But today it is primarily a room for display, because of the fragility of many of its contents, not least the rare Isfahan carpet, which dates from the 16th or early 17th century.

Two quite different styles of Boulle writing desk can be seen here. At either end is a kneehole desk, or *bureau Mazarin*, with red-backed tortoiseshell and brass marquetry, dating from early in the Louis XIV period. Compact and almost fussy, these desks contrast with the later, more elegant *bureau plat* in the centre, the work of André-Charles Boulle himself, which dates from around 1710.

Out of sight here are the console tables, with their marble tops supported by giltwood dolphins, attributed to the decorative team of Henry Flitcroft and Benjamin Goodison, c.1740. The William and Mary winged armchairs in the corners have their original and rare red-faded-to-green covers. Also original are the velvet covers of the Charles II chairs on either side of the fireplace, with their distinctive curved backs. The triple-arched overmantel was the creation of the 2nd Duke, using recycled woodwork.

The tapestries, with their bacchanalian scenes of young boys playing amid fountains and grapes, are Flemish and date from c.1665. The intertwined spotted snakes that form the borders are said to symbolise immortality.

ABOVE *A Meissen swan by JJ Kaendler in a reed stand by J-C Duplessis, c.1750, one of pair that may have belonged to Madame de Pompadour*
ABOVE LEFT CLAUDE LEFÈBVRE (1632–1675) OR HIS FATHER, JEAN LEFÈBVRE (1600–1675)
Louis XIV (r.1643–1715)
A miniature of the Sun King holding a baton
LEFT NICOLAS LAVREINCE THE YOUNGER (1737–1807)
Marie Antoinette (1755–93)
A miniature by the Stockholm-born artist. This was probably purchased, along with the portrait of Louis XIV, by the 5th Duke and Duchess of Buccleuch as part of their great miniature collection, now at Bowhill

FAR LEFT *The 24ft-long Isfahan carpet, with its burgundy ground and pale-blue palmettes, is early 17th-century and was acquired by Duke Ralph*
LEFT *One of the ormolu masks on André-Charles Boulle's elegant 'bureau plat', c.1710*
BELOW *The Rainbow Room was known as 'the Rainbow Sleeping Room' in 1801. Bedrooms were often named after a salient feature of a tapestry hanging in them, though no rainbow tapestry has been identified. The four here are Flemish and from the same set as those in the Duke's Study (page 82)*

The Morning Room

With its comfortable sofas and mellow tones, this has become Boughton's principal sitting room. Its windows look both into the Fish Court and down the avenue to the Broad Water

People sink almost irretrievably into the rather faded crimson sofas of this family sitting room. The floors both here and in the Rainbow Room were replaced in 1976 by Boughton's own craftsmen, using oak that had been growing on the estate for over 300 years. The need for this replacement is emphasised by some alarming deathwatch-beetle damage displayed in the doorway between the two rooms.

The tapestries of bacchanalian scenes belong to one of two sets at Boughton known as *The Naked Boys*, woven at Mortlake in the 1670s from drawings by Raphael's pupil Giulio Romano (c.1499–1546). The Mortlake St George's Cross has been woven into the right-hand margin. In a panel near the door to the Drawing Room, one of the little boys can be seen misbehaving from a tree.

Between the windows looking down the avenue is a portrait of Duke John's elder brother, Winwood (page 142), painted in Paris in 1699 during his Grand Tour, with a fine frame in the style of William Kent. Winwood died three years later in Hanover, supposedly of alcohol poisoning.

When recitals are not being staged in the Great Hall, this is the home of a beautiful harpsichord built by Andrew Garlick in 2010 (page 200) Early musical instruments sit on either side of a silverpoint drawing of musicians in a court scene (overleaf). Research to identify the harpsichord player is in progress: it has been speculated that it might be the young Mozart, who toured the great cities of Europe in 1765–66.

LEFT *The Morning Room, a haven of ease between the Rainbow Room and the more stiffly formal Drawing Room*

RIGHT *For a century a copy of Van Dyck's portrait of Charles I's children has hung over the fire, between the Mortlake 'Naked Boys' tapestries*

ABOVE UNKNOWN ARTIST,
18TH CENTURY
A music party
*Family tradition has long held that
the harpsichordist in this silverpoint
drawing is the young Mozart. This
may be wishful thinking*

LEFT CIRCLE OF FRANÇOIS
DE TROY (1645–1730)
**Winwood Montagu, Viscount
Monthermer (1682–1702)**
*The 2nd Duke's elder brother in
long, flowing wig, painted in Paris
in 1699 during an ambitious
Grand Tour. He died three years
later at the court of the
future George I in Hanover*

RIGHT JEAN-BAPTISTE MONNOYER
(1636–99)
Flowers in a bronze bowl
*A fine flower painting, with parrot
tulips (the red-and-white one recalls
the tulip 'Estelle Rijnveld'), a single
white-and-yellow tazetta daffodil and
three white bells of Summer Snowflake,
'Leucojum aestivum'. The Huguenot
Monnoyer came to England with Ralph
Montagu in 1678 and 52 paintings by
him were recorded in a 1709 inventory*

The Drawing Room

The original Tudor parlour is now an understated showcase for two of Boughton's treasures: a rare Elizabethan carpet, perhaps the oldest woven in England, and dozens of Van Dyck grisaille portraits

Once a 16th-century parlour, then a dining room, the subtly elegant Drawing Room is now firmly centred round the stone fireplace, brought here in 1910 from Hemington, the Northamptonshire house of the 1st Sir Edward Montagu's father. Directly below it is a rug of great historical interest, one of a set of four that may be the earliest extant carpets woven in England. Three bear coats of arms with the Montagu lozenges; on the flatweave ends of two are the dates 1584 and 1585 (page 13).

Displayed in vertical groupings around the room are a set of 40 grisaille portraits by Sir Anthony van Dyck. They were painted in oil on oak panels so that they could then be engraved for his *Iconography*, published in 1645. These portraits of distinguished figures in the Netherlands and England included his

LEFT This Tudor fireplace came from another Montagu manor in 1910. In front of it is one of Boughton's four 16th-century 'Turkey rugs' – the Montagu arms can be seen in the border. On the far left, next to the Louis XV sofa, is a 'bonheur du jour' (lady's writing desk), mounted with Sèvres plaques, by Martin Carlin, 1768
RIGHT One of a pair of very rare 17th-century japanned 'India Cabinets', once thought to be European but now believed to be Japanese. They were in Montagu House, Bloomsbury, in 1707, and may have travelled to Jamaica with Ralph's future second wife, the Duchess of Albemarle

friends and patrons – among them Rubens and Charles I. They belonged to his successor, Sir Peter Lely, Principal Painter in Ordinary to Charles II, from whose sale in 1682 they were bought by Ralph Montagu.

The tulipwood writing table (c.1760) by Joseph Baumhauer (opposite) has 24 small square Sèvres plaques mounted round its edge. The practice of combining porcelain and furniture was refined by makers such as Martin Carlin, whose *bonheur du jour*, dated 1768, is mounted with 17 fine Sèvres plaques in 10 irregular shapes (page 144). These desks show how far fashions had moved in a century from Pierre Gole's marquetry desk in the Low Pavilion Anteroom (page 81).

Daniel Marot is credited with the design of the pair of bucolic mirrors fitted with stands to hold flower vases or candlesticks, although they were probably created and gilded by Jean Pelletier in 1691 for Ralph Montagu. The sofas and chairs are Louis XV, some of them bearing the stamp of JJ Pothier.

HEV MIHI QVIA INCOLAT' ME PROLO
GATVS EST

LEFT *Joseph Baumhauer's early-1760s 'bureau plat' inset with Sèvres porcelain was acquired by the 5th Duke of Buccleuch in 1830. Above it are portraits of Mary Montagu, wife of the 3rd Duke, in old age by Francis Cotes (1726–70), and as a young woman by John Giles Eccardt (1720–79)*
BELOW *The Drawing Room in 1876, when it was full of Victorian clutter. The interior designer John Fowler imposed order in the 1950s*

LEFT FRENCH SCHOOL
A Young Lady, late 16th century
This soulful portrait, thought to be Mary, Queen of Scots, bears the words from Psalm 119, 'Woe is me, that my sojourning is prolonged!'
FAR LEFT CIRCLE OF JACOB OOST THE YOUNGER (1639–1713)
A boy thought to be the future William III
RIGHT ATTRIBUTED TO
ANDREA SACCHI (1599–1661)
Portrait of Claude Lorrain (c.1600–1682)
The great landscape painter kept this portrait from the 1630s until his death, leaving a copy to the Accademia di San Luca in Rome in his will
FAR RIGHT SIR ANTHONY VAN DYCK (1599–1641)
Self-Portrait
One of the portraits painted by Van Dyck on oak panels 'en grisaille' for engravers to work from in preparing his 'Iconography', a book of portraits published posthumously in 1645 (see overleaf)

Adriaen Brouwer, genre painter

Peter Paul Rubens, painter

King Charles I

Diego de Guzmán, commander

Frederick Henry, Prince of Orange

A daughter of Philip II of Spain

Geneviève, Duchesse de Croÿ

Carlos Coloma, Marqués de la Espina

Nicolas-Claude Fabri de Peiresc

Cornelis van der Geest, merchant

Gaston, Duc d'Orléans, Henri IV's son

Jan van Ravesteyn, painter

Cornelis van der Geest, merchant

Simon de Vos, artist

Justus Lipsius, philosopher

Adam de Coster, artist

Amalia, Princess of Orange

Gaspar de Crayer, artist

Frans Francken the Younger, artist

'PICTURES IN CHIAROSCURE'
Hanging in neat columns in the Drawing Room are grisailles associated with the 'Iconography', a book of portraits Van Dyck was working on at the time of his death in 1641. Ralph Montagu paid £115 for 37 in the 1682 Lely sale. All but four of the 41 at Boughton are thought to be by Van Dyck himself. After they vanished in a fire at Montagu House in 1686, a notice in 'The London Gazette' offered £10 for their recovery

A Gentleman

Ambrogio Spinola, condottiere

Jan Caspar Gevaerts, jurist and poet

Paul Pontius, engraver

Cardinal–Infante Ferdinand of Spain

Sebastian Vrancx, painter

Count de Feria, soldier and diplomat

Marten Pepijn, artist

Peeter de Jode, engraver

Artus Wolfaerdt, artist

Peter Stevens, connoisseur

Anton Cornelissen, connoisseur

Andreas Colyns de Nole, sculptor

Peter Paul Rubens, painter

Hendrik van Balen, artist

Adriaen van Stalbemt, artist

Marqués de Santa Cruz, general

Karel van Mallery, engraver

Graf von Pappenheim, general

Artus Wolfaerdt, artist

The Library

A tranquil, very English room, the Library – once part of the Tudor Great Chamber – is characteristic of Duke John's taste in interiors, displaying his love of antiquity, heraldry and genealogy

Directly above the Drawing Room is one of the most frequently used yet most tranquil rooms in the house. For the present Duke's parents, the Library was a refuge, the place to retire for peaceful evenings with a blazing fire and the television, right beside their bedroom in the Flower Gallery. With windows facing east over the courtyard – the only ones in the Tudor style to survive – and facing west over the Broad Water, this room captures the light at both ends of the day.

The George II tiered bookcases, with their scrollwork and foliage carvings, satyrs'

ABOVE *Duke John greatly admired the Wingfield family portrait between the George II mahogany bookcases. Until 1948 other bookcases obscured the Tudor windows. The oval-backed chairs are William and Mary* RIGHT *Harking back to the Tudor with its barrel vaulting, small-square panelling and heraldic chimneypiece, Duke John's Library is in marked contrast to his father's oak-panelled halls, still fashionable in the 1690s. Originally part of the Great Chamber, this room was first described as a library in 1730*

LEFT CIRCLE OF CHARLES PHILIPS (1708–47)
Group portrait with Francis Scott, 2nd Duke of Buccleuch (1695–1751)
The 2nd Duke is seen in a blue coat with a silver-braided red vest and the Riband of the Order of the Thistle
BOTTOM LEFT *A panel from the late-16th-century set of tapestries in the Flower Gallery Passage depicting Judith and Holofernes*
BOTTOM RIGHT MICHIEL VAN MUSSCHER (1645–1705)
Portrait of Jeronimus Velters, his wife, Catherina Tielens, and their daughter Helena
The chimneypiece in this portrait bears the arms of the Tielens of Amsterdam and the Velters. It was described as Lord Monthermer's property when Richard Godfrey made an engraving of it in 1769

OPPOSITE, MAIN PICTURE ENGLISH SCHOOL, 17TH CENTURY
Portrait of a child, possibly Charles, Prince of Wales
Paintings of children in the Nursery include one said to depict the future Charles II. He wears a white-lace-edged dress and cap, and holds a coral rattle. A parrot pecks at the sprig of cherries in his hand
TOP RIGHT WILLIAM INGALTON
Walter Francis, 5th Duke of Buccleuch (1806–84), and Lord John Scott (1809–84)
The 5th Duke and his brother at Eton
BOTTOM RIGHT
JAMES STEVENSON HARVEY
Eton and Windsor, 1821
A record of the flood of December 27, 1821, painted by the archivist at Windsor Castle

THE SOUTH SIDE
A quiet corner

As you look down on the house from the Rose Garden and the Lily Pond, Boughton takes on the air of a small village. Adjoining the West Front, the South Side was transformed by Duke John into the house's sunniest living quarters in the early 1740s. What was once a chapel became the main drawing room

The South Side of the house appears to be at least as old as the Great Hall. In early Tudor times it was a long, independent building of two storeys. Not until 1579–80 was it joined to the main manor house. There were lodgings for the family and an apartment known as the 'King's Room'. The open timber ceilings, which have purlins with heavy mouldings, are now concealed by 17th-century plaster vaults.

A Tudor chapel dedicated to St John the Baptist was converted into living quarters by Duke John, who extensively remodelled the

ABOVE *The South Side, with a jumble of rooftops beyond. The White Drawing Room (overleaf) occupies the first floor. The uppermost windows belong to the attics of the North Front*

South Side in 1741–43. The upper part of the chapel is now the White Drawing Room.

As with the West Front, the South Side continued to evolve in the 20th and 21st centuries; walls were moved and new bathrooms created. With its sunny aspect and views over the Rose Garden and up to the Lily Pond, it has long been a favourite living space for the family. The 8th Duke's widow, Mollie, had her apartments here for many years, and the Nursery returned to the southwest corner, where it had been in Duke John's day and where it makes a perfect vantage point over comings and goings.

LEFT The southwest corner of Boughton, seen from the path to the Rose Garden, where the grass is encouraged to grow long. The window on the left, overlooking syringa bushes, belongs to the Nursery, which was created in 1718 at the end of the Elizabethan Long Gallery

The White Drawing Room

Upstairs, at eye level with the Rose Garden, is one of the most pleasing rooms at Boughton. The panelling and heraldic touches are evidence of the 2nd Duke's hand

In addition to the Nursery in the southwest corner of the South Side, there are three other first-floor rooms overlooking the Rose Garden: Duke Walter's Bedroom, the White Drawing Room and, at the end, the Armorial Sitting Room.

All the rooms have the distinctive small-square panelling mentioned in a letter to the Duke John by his chief steward John Booth. And there are yet more heraldic overmantels. The colourful one in the Armorial Sitting Room (top left, overleaf) celebrates the Montagu descent from Edward I and Eleanor of Castile, though the central coat of arms, bearing the motto ÆQUITAS ACTIONUM REGULA ('Let equity rule our actions'), is the 2nd Duke's own.

Accounts show that he transformed the chapel into the White Drawing Room – William Green was paid for 'lathing and plastering the chapel' and for 'slating where the new chimney is put up in the chapel'. From January to March 1730 Boughton labourers were working 'for the new apartment', making flooring and other 'joinery work about the new alterations, partitions, wainscoting, doors'. In all, they apparently cut '600 firs'.

These are the rooms most often occupied by the family, along with the bedrooms below, off the South Passage. Light and airy, they contain a mix of traditional and more modern furnishings and works of art, including paintings by notable Scottish artists such as Elizabeth Blackadder and Alberto Morrocco.

LEFT *Duke John added his favourite Tudor touches – small-square panelling and a heraldic chimneypiece – when he converted this vaulted room. The tapestry at the far end is based on a painting by the Scottish artist Victoria Crowe, woven by the Dovecote Tapestry Company in Edinburgh in 2011. Between the windows is 'Lake Avernus', one of two Claudian views in this room by Richard Wilson, the 18th-century father of British landscape painting. It has recently come to light that it was acquired by Charlotte Anne, 5th Duchess of Buccleuch, in 1840, having previously belonged to the artist Constable, a gift from his patron Sir George Beaumont*

ABOVE RICHARD WILSON, RA (1714–82)
**The Villa Medici, Rome, with imaginary
surroundings, 1752**
*Detail of a work bought by Monthermer in Rome.
Thomas Jenkins, Wilson's friend and principal
agent, was instrumental in many of his purchases*
RIGHT *Duke John's heraldic griffin and Garter
above the White Drawing Room fireplace*
TOP *The overmantel in the adjoining Armorial
Sitting Room celebrates the Montagus' descent
from Edward I and Eleanor of Castile*

The Chinese Staircase

The eastern end of the South Side reveals a jumble of quite major alterations over the years, and includes the lovely Chinese Staircase, installed by Duke John in 1743. This must be the one identified in a letter of 1763 by Horace Walpole, one of the earliest writers about country houses: 'There were nothing but pedigrees all around me and under my feet, for there is literally a coat of arms at the end of every step of the stairs – did the Duke mean to pun, and intend this for the *descent* of the Montagus?'

The staircase, known simply as the 'Brown Staircase' in early records, is beside the South Door entrance used by the family, which gives access to the Old and New Kitchens and also to the Audit Room and the South Passage.

ABOVE JEAN-BAPTISTE MONNOYER
Flowers in a sculpted urn, 1698
LEFT *The joiner Humphrey Blofield used recycled wood for the Chinese Staircase in 1743. His deal balustrade was replaced in oak in 1939. Montagu lozenges appear in the specially woven carpet*

The Audit Room

The Audit Room, with its vivid silk wedding banners and shovelboard table, was the final addition to the Fish Court. Farm tenants came here to pay their rent – and to be plied with strong drink from Boughton's brewhouse

The South Door also served as a one-time 'office' entrance, giving quick access to what was probably the last major piece of construction at Boughton, the Audit Room, built in 1746–47. It is also one of the most surprising, running for 84 feet, almost the whole length of the east side of the Fish Court. With its 62 heraldic shields around the walls, it was the last flourish of the Montagu interest in heraldry. The Tudor fireplace bears the arms of the first Sir Edward and must have come from another part of the house. It has engaging inscriptions, one in Latin, NE SIS ARGUS FORIS ET DOMI TALPA ('Do not be a peacock abroad and a mole at home'), and another in French, MILLE DOULEURS POUR UNE PLEASOIR ('A thousand sorrows for one pleasure').

The room was originally 'the music gallery' but, as the name suggests, it was here that farm tenants came to settle their accounts and would traditionally have been entertained. Recently identified on the back of a pewter plate is a charming inscription by a tenant in nearby Warkton village, which reads: 'Charles Panther used me at Lady Day Audit 1799 and did very well indeed'.

Running down the centre of the room is the long shovelboard table, the work in 1704 of Roger Davis, the principal house joiner. Players slid weighty brass coins from the far end, aiming to reach a predetermined spot without ending up in the gulley traps along the edges. Only one other example of such a table, at Stanway in Gloucestershire, home of the Earl of Wemyss, is known to survive.

Brought out only for the most special occasions are the 23 pale-green silk banners made for the wedding of Duke John and Mary Churchill, the Duke of Marlborough's daughter, in 1705. They owe their remarkable condition to having been hidden away in a chest and forgotten for more than 250 years.

The Audit Room provides a splendid portrait gallery, but inevitably the eye is caught by the displays of Vincennes and Sèvres porcelain.

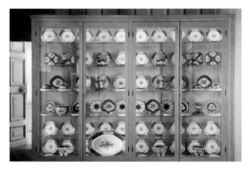

ABOVE *A cabinet in the Audit Room displaying a Louis XV Sèvres dinner service dated 1753–56*
RIGHT *The spectacular silk banners were carried at the wedding of Duke John and Lady Mary Churchill in 1705. The shovelboard table took 29 days to build in 1704 at a cost of £3 17s 4d*

The Sèvres porcelain

Much of the Audit Room's Sèvres was made for Louis XV and two famous mistresses. The 5th Duke built the collection in less than two years

Boughton's Sèvres porcelain collection is almost entirely the creation of Walter Francis, 5th Duke of Buccleuch, and his wife, Charlotte Anne. Throughout their lives together they were prodigious collectors of paintings, furniture and rare books. Shortly after their marriage in 1829, they became entranced by Sèvres porcelain, and for 18 months they became obsessive buyers, with the help of the dealer Edward Holmes Baldock, who supplied original pieces, sometimes enlarging or enhancing them with gilded bronze mounts or additional painted decoration.

The break-up of the French royal collections and those of the aristocracy after the revolutionary turmoil at the end of the 18th century created enormous opportunities for wealthy British buyers, and some of the finest Sèvres collections today – such as those in the Wallace Collection and in the British Royal Collection – were formed or enlarged in the first half of the 19th century.

High-quality porcelain had become hugely valued in Europe following large importations from China and Japan in the 17th century. In Europe, particularly in France, efforts were made for decades to emulate it with relatively unsatisfactory forms of soft-paste porcelain. The establishment of the Meissen factory in 1710 by Augustus II, Elector of Saxony, marked the first successful European attempt to replicate the secret mixture of feldspar and kaolin known as hard-paste porcelain, which was fired at very high temperatures and decorated. It gave such prestige to rulers of Saxony that it was known as 'white gold'.

It was not until the establishment of a factory at Vincennes, the precursor to Sèvres, in 1740, that significant advances were made in the production of soft-paste porcelain, with its creamy, more tactile appeal and thick glazes. The Vincennes enterprise was supported by Louis XV's mistress Madame de Pompadour and her friends. The famous cypher trademark – crossed Ls for 'Louis' (overleaf) – was established in 1751. Later a code letter was added to signify the year of manufacture – hitherto

One of a pair of vases for flowers, bulbs and potpourri, 1758/59, with later gilt-bronze mounts. Decorated by the celebrated figure painter Charles-Nicolas Dodin, it is probably part of a garniture bought by Louis XV's mistress, Madame de Pompadour

A plate ordered by Madame du Barry, with the initials D in gilding and B in flowers, from a large service that was unfinished on Louis XV's death in 1774. The King's last mistress was unable to pay for its completion

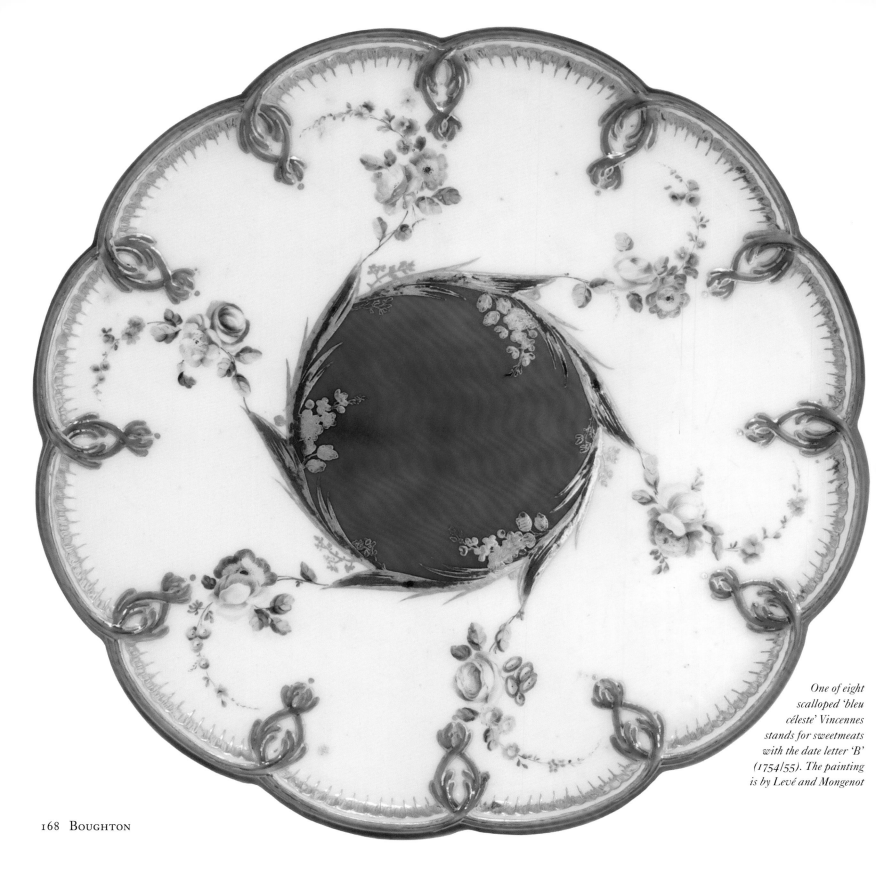

One of eight scalloped 'bleu céleste' Vincennes stands for sweetmeats with the date letter 'B' (1754/55). The painting is by Levé and Mongenot

believed to be A for 1753, B for 1754 and so on, although recent research by David Peters, an authority on Sèvres, argues that the starting date should be 1754 rather than 1753. In 1756 the factory moved to its present home in Sèvres and three years later it was bought by the King.

The earliest pieces on display at Boughton, plates made for the huge dinner service created for Louis XV over an eight-year period, show the letter A, while the latest (apart from fabrications by Baldock) come from the 1790s and have the letters RF, denoting their manufacture during the early years of the République Française.

Boughton is particularly rich in pieces from Louis XV's dinner service, made in the magnificent turquoise colour known as *bleu céleste*. As well as dinner plates, there are serving dishes in all kinds of shapes reflecting the menus of the time – ice-cream cups; basins with a Catherine-wheel effect for sweetmeats; dishes for marzipans, sugared almonds and the like; and huge meat platters, an extraordinary technical achievement when it came to the firing process.

From flower and potpourri vases to toilet basins and tea sets, these were items for the most refined living in court and aristocratic circles, and were created at huge expense with outstanding style and artistic skill.

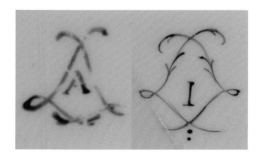

LEFT *The crossed Ls for 'Louis' adopted as the Vincennes and Sèvres trademark in 1751. The date letter 'A' represents 1753/54 and 'I', 1761/62*
TOP LEFT AND ABOVE *One of four 'bleu céleste' shell dishes (top) and a mortier (above) from Louis XV's dinner service, both with the date letter 'A'. Mortiers were used for mixing fruit and spices for a drink and often paired with a punchbowl*
ABOVE RIGHT *A pair of vases 'd'après l'ancien' with the date letter 'F' (1758/59). Before David Peters' research into letter dating, these vases were thought to have been presented by the factory to the painter François Boucher in June 1758*
TOP RIGHT AND RIGHT *Sèvres birds and a 'rose marbré' flowerpot, both with the date letter 'I'*

The working house

The functional core of the house, with its Steward's Hall, Servants' Hall and Kitchen, revolved around the Clock Court. A labyrinth of corridors, staircases and doorways provided access to the rest of the house

When you stand in the Clock Court, you are at the heart of the eerily silent engine room of the great house. Above, from within a simple metal frame high on the steeply pitched roof, a chiming bell maintains the rhythm of the household. Three centuries ago, when scores of people were employed and entertaining was in full swing, it would have been a bustling hubbub, a hive of industry filled with smells and noises.

In a corner is the door to the Kitchen, still very much in use today, with its solid iron range at one end and an only slightly less ancient Aga at the other, surmounted by a rotating spit mechanism from an altogether different era. Around the walls run gleaming coppers, pots and pans of all sizes, and moulds for mousses and jellies in a profusion of decorative shapes.

A low doorway led to the adjoining Servants' Hall for the kitchen maids, scullery boys and junior valets, where they could eat at the long oak tables and spend their few spare moments. Beyond it was the Bucket Hall, where the rudimentary equipment for dealing with the ever-present threat of fire was stored: leather buckets filled with sand, and an antique fire engine with unwieldy brass and leather hoses.

Upstairs, beneath the eaves, the Long Room would have offered tolerably warm sleeping

THE TUDOR KITCHEN
ABOVE *A bell on the roof rings on the hour in the Clock Court. The white door leads to what has been the Kitchen since 16th century*
LEFT *One end of the Kitchen is now a convivial dining room, with a high scrubbed oak 17th-century refectory table, an old iron range at one end, and a wall of gleaming copper*

ABOVE AND RIGHT *Each piece of copper is inscribed DBQ (Duke of Buccleuch and Queensberry) along with the initials of the house it belonged to: MH for Montagu House, BH for Boughton House, R for Richmond (the villa on the Thames bought by the 3rd Duchess of Montagu)*

OPPOSITE, LEFT *The Clock Court and its Tudor clock. The pendulum built into the house drops to the ground floor*
RIGHT *The Kitchen's early-19th-century oak-case clock, by Merrill of Richmond, with its painted dial*

quarters, thanks to the heat from the stoves, baking ovens and open fires below.

At a discreet remove from all of this, but also looking into the Clock Court, lay the rather grander Steward's Hall, for the senior members of the ducal household, with its massive Jacobean fireplace and commanding position. Today this has become an occasional exhibition space and a venue for small receptions and dinners, especially when there are concerts in the Great Hall. This new function has revealed how central the Steward's Hall was to the self-sufficient community that a great house had become by the 18th century.

One door gives access to what one might call 'front of house', either directly into the Egyptian Hall, or via the discreet corridor behind the Great Hall leading to the Staircase Hall. Just through another lay the external steps to the courtyard in front of the Stables. Adjacent were two staircases: the steep, narrow Footman's Stairs, rising to the top of

the house, and the gentler, broader Lime Staircase. The former surely derived their name from being the back stairs by which staff reached the rooms of those they were there to serve. Recently they have attracted a local lustre for having featured in the 2012 film of the musical *Les Misérables*.

The Lime Staircase (page 178) feels very fine for something that was the preserve of the domestic staff – a status it no longer has in the 21st century. Its carved balusters were renewed about 50 years ago from lime trees grown on the estate, providing its name and the subtle scent that pervades it.

Historic houses, despite their size, are often poorly equipped with suitable space for special collections. At Boughton the simplest storage spaces for furniture are provided by the former staff sleeping quarters, including the Long Room, which runs off the Lime Staircase at a mezzanine level. The Servants' Hall beside the Kitchen is now the Armoury (page 182), and a row of former bedrooms on the first floor is now the preserve of the Archivist and student researchers.

Right Vincenzo Campi (c.1536–1591)
A market girl by a vegetable stall
Though this painting was once attributed to Joachim Beuckelaer, the theatrical perspective, Cremona basket, the crisp folds of the dress and the flowers (perhaps here a vanitas symbol) all point to the Italian Mannerist
Above left Anthony Leemans (c.1636–71/77)
Still life with falconry implements, 1658
The 2nd Lord Montagu, who owned this painting in the Colonnade Passage, was a keen falconer. A bill from his 'hawker', William Deone, survives in the archives
Left *The steps in the Colonnade Passage are part of the North Front's formal entrance to the Great Hall*

ABOVE *The Lion Court, home to Duke John's toothless lion after its retirement from the zoo in the Tower of London. He befriended it when he had his offices at the Tower as Master-General of the Ordnance* ABOVE RIGHT *A knife sharpener in the passage to the lantern-roofed room where meat and fish were smoked* RIGHT *The Steward's Hall, 1740–41, with its Jacobean overmantel* OPPOSITE *This panelled vestibule outside the Steward's Hall joins the working house to the house of grand entertaining. To the left is the Egyptian Hall. The door in the centre leads to the Footman's Stairs and on to the North Front*

ABOVE *The discreet way to the top of the house is by the narrow Footmen's Stairs that link the Steward's Hall to the Attics, passing the unofficial State Bedroom hidden behind the State Rooms*

OPPOSITE *The Lime Staircase was built in 1718–19 by Hugh Franklin, from a local family of joiners, when Duke John added an attic floor to the Unfinished Wing. Unsettlingly much wider at the top than at the bottom, it leads from the Bucket Hall past the door to the Fifth State Room. Generations of Franklins remained close to the Montagus. The 3rd Duke helped Hugh's grandson to escape military service overseas in 1756; a charming letter from the boy's parents thanking him is in the archives*

RIGHT *Three of the House Ladies, who tirelessly keep dust and cobwebs at bay and the furniture gleaming with beeswax, line up on the West Attic Staircase. From left to right: Brenda Chapman, Norma Weekley and Julie Jackson*

LEFT THE PRINT ROOM
All the family have been voracious collectors of prints, but the 3rd Duke and Duchess were among the first to hang them on walls as a style of interior decoration, at their villa in Richmond (page 36). The Buccleuchs also commissioned prints of family portraits for circulation – an early instance of PR management, as used on an unprecedented scale by the Duke of Monmouth to prepare the public for his bid to succeed his father, Charles II

ABOVE *The 16th-century gable wall of the Great Hall's roof. The hatch provides access to the original Tudor vaulted ceiling*

ABOVE RIGHT *The corridor linking the Attics of the Northwest and Northeast Pavilions. These dining chairs saw years of use in the Great Hall after it became the main dining room in 1911*

RIGHT *The glass panes displayed in this attic passage were painted with coats of arms for Duke John, forever passionate about matters heraldic. They include the Brudenell arms, so they must have been painted after his daughter's marriage to Lord Cardigan, the future 3rd Duke, in 1730. They may also have been intended for use in the Great Hall*

ABOVE *A servant's bedroom at the top of the Footman's Stairs, with an ebony bed from Ceylon or Batavia, carved with the coat of arms of Col. John Fitzgerald, Governor of Tangier 1664–65*
RIGHT *The present Duke stands beside a mirror from Montagu House, Whitehall, and rolled-up tapestries sealed against light and moths*

The Dower House and the Stables

The façades of these buildings completed Duke Ralph's vision of an urbane château. But turn the corner, and below the Collyweston slates, dressed stone gives way to warm, rust-coloured brickwork

The relatively simple building beyond the Unfinished Wing, which continues the North Front as far as the Stables, has come to be known as the Dower House, although it has served a variety of purposes over the centuries, including that of the house laundry.

The Montagu heiress Elizabeth Montagu, widow of Henry, 3rd Duke of Buccleuch, occasionally occupied it until her death in 1827, hence the building's name. Later in that century it became the home of the 5th Duke of Buccleuch's younger brother Admiral Lord Charles Scott and his family, and then of the

RIGHT *The walls of Boughton at the back are entirely of brick. The Dower House stands in its own garden on the left, next to the Stables. On the right is the Brewhouse*
BELOW *The Stables (left) and Dower House (right) from the north, with the late Duchess Jane's herbaceous border*

Admiral's son, Sir David Scott, who lived to the age of 99. His widow, the well-known gardener and garden photographer Valerie Finnis, was the most recent occupant. His only son, Merlin, died in the Second World War at the age of 22, and after her death in 2007 his remarkable art collection, including Victorian paintings bought long before they became fashionable, was sold to endow the Finnis Scott Foundation, which makes grants in the areas of horticulture and plant sciences as well as fine art and art history, and the Merlin Trust, set up to encourage young horticulturalists.

Like the Dower House, the imposing stable block added to the North Front by Duke Ralph in 1704–05 is faced in the same dressed Weldon stone used in the main house (right). The pediment was carved in 1705 by Gideon du Chesne, who noted: 'I sett out from London for my Lord Duke's House at Boughton and there

did cutt my Lord Dukes Coat of arms which stand over the stables being in length twenty foot.' The cost was £15. Invisible from the front, the east side is built in simpler red brick, fired in the park near the village of Weekley.

In the late 1970s the Stables came close to collapse, as a result of seepage of water from a culvert running beneath them, which over the centuries had undermined the foundations. The uneven movement of the building has resulted in cracks and distortions that can still be seen clearly within and to the right of the archway. Complex restoration work was undertaken, involving underpinning the foundations, while steel and concrete frames were inserted at the top of the building to hold it together.

The interior has been adapted and now houses, on the ground floor, a tearoom, a gift shop and the magnificent family State Coach, built in 1830. Upstairs, in the loft, the new Tapestry Suite provides a space for events and an occasional gallery. Much of the plasterwork has been left in place, with its graffiti by generations of grooms and stable boys.

OPPOSITE *The Stables, seen from the back drive (top) and from an attic window (bottom)*
LEFT *Sir David Scott and his wife Valerie Finnis in the Dower House, photographed by Norman Parkinson for Vogue in 1976*
ABOVE AND RIGHT *The State Coach, with the Buccleuch arms and black and yellow livery, was built in 1830 by Samuel Hobbs of Barker & Co. In 1907 they built the first Silver Ghost for Rolls-Royce*

The Archives

This wide-ranging private collection of historic documents, dating back to the 12th century, still has a wealth of secrets to reveal

The Montagu Archives are extensive and complex, reflecting a web of family relationships and connections. They also interlock with the archives of the Dukes of Buccleuch in Scotland, the earliest documents of which date back to around 1130.

The contents are often tangential. Surprisingly, for example, the papers of another duke, the Duke of Shrewsbury, when Secretary of State, are found in the archives, because the 3rd Duke of Montagu's father, Lord Cardigan, was his cousin and executor. The Dukes of Albemarle also feature prominently, because the widow of the 2nd and last Duke married Ralph Montagu. As

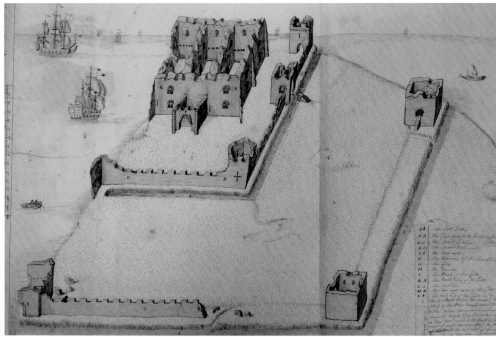

if to complete a circle, they include letters concerning the 2nd Duke of Albemarle's West Country campaign in 1685 against the Duke of Buccleuch's ancestor the Duke of Monmouth.

Part of the archives is currently on loan to the Northamptonshire Record Office, while the remainder is spread through the house and in the Archive Office, where Crispin Powell, the Archivist, works alongside a number of postgraduate students. The archive research has been enormously helped by generous support from the University of Huddersfield and by a collaborative project with the University of Leicester.

ABOVE *The medieval castle on Piel Island, inherited by the 2nd Duke from his stepmother, the Duchess of Albemarle. In 1920 the 7th Duke of Buccleuch gave it to the authorities as a memorial to those who lost their lives in the First World War*
LEFT *A treatise on improving cannon by the Master Gunner of Calais after the sinking of the 'Mary Rose' in 1545, probably acquired by the 2nd Duke when he was in charge of the Ordnance*
TOP RIGHT *Three volumes of bills were presented by the Pelletier family after the 1st Duke's death, including 'mending Oliver Cromwell's picture'*
RIGHT *The Archivist, Crispin Powell, unfolds the gardener Leonard van der Meulen's 1709 contract*

The archives date from the 12th century, covering 900 years of history. The earliest documents concern land purchases, but these are quickly joined by a rich seam of manorial records, illuminating the lives of ordinary people. The main barrier to unlocking these records is that the scribes used Latin and abbreviations.

There are letters and accounts, both personal and official, the latter focused on the many public offices held by the family. From Elizabethan and Jacobean times, we have records of the local militia, and the papers of Duke Ralph's grandfather Sir Ralph Winwood as a diplomat and politician. Then there are the 1st Lord Montagu's parliamentary journals in the lead-up to the Civil War. We have Ralph Montagu's letters as ambassador to France under Charles II.

From the 18th century, there are many papers generated by the 2nd Duke's job heading the Board of Ordnance, a volume on his expedition to colonise the Caribbean, and another concerning his revival of the Order

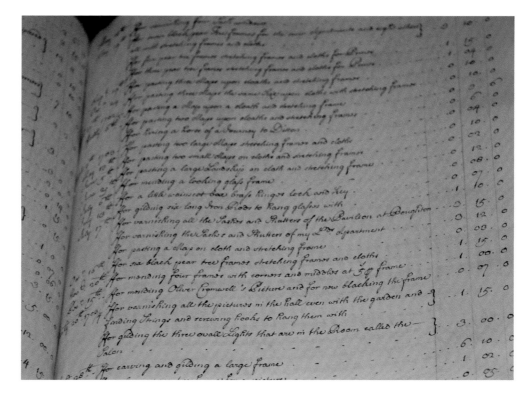

of the Bath. The Duke also kept wonderful battle plans for his father-in-law Marlborough's campaigns and collected military treatises, such as one for the improvement of Henry VIII's cannon. There are vivid and amusing letters by Henry Lyte, tutor to Lord Monthermer, on his pupil's Grand Tour of 1751–60. From the reign of George III, we have papers of the 3rd Duke of Montagu, the King's friend and governor to his sons, including his private accounts.

There are estate papers, stewards' letters and hundreds of volumes of accounts and rentals concerning lands in Northamptonshire, Warwickshire, Hampshire, Lancashire, Buckinghamshire and elsewhere. They touch on the lives of the tenants, servants and tradesmen connected to the Montagus.

Letters for the Boughton estate under the 2nd Duke are published by the Northamptonshire Record Society. People and

landscapes are given a colourful setting by maps and surveys, which run from 1604 and reach their pinnacle under the 2nd Duke with a beautiful series created by his steward John Booth and by William Brasier. Relief maps of part of the Lake District are also remarkable.

The great houses are described by inventories, from 1684, and by architectural drawings. The running of the household under the 2nd Duke is charted by accounts, regulations for servants and 'bills of fare', tabulating the food and drink consumed at meals and the numbers fed. Household and executors' accounts cover the lavish lifestyle of his father, Duke Ralph.

It will take years of patient study to get the full measure of the rich material, but for future generations it will offer some of the most fascinating opportunities for enjoying and understanding the collections.

The Montagu Music Collection

This unique archive at Boughton includes exquisite first-edition classical manuscripts, extremely rare scores for old English musicals, and even instructions for long-forgotten dances

The Montagu Music Collection reveals the changing styles and uses of music, both publicly and in the home, from the 16th to the early 19th century. In all it comprises more than 500 volumes of music.

Many of the volumes are true masterpieces of the art of printing, with elaborately engraved title pages, portraits and dedications – visually beautiful in their own right, before we even consider the musical content. Some of the Italian madrigal volumes from the 1590s

OPPOSITE *A dance from Lully's 'Armide', from the Le Rousseau 'Collection of Dances' by the 2nd Duke's dancing master, Anthony L'Abbé (1667–1758), published in London in 1720. The French notation method, established in the 1680s, remained in use throughout the 18th century*

BELOW *One of England's earliest books of printed music, 'Recueil du Mellange', by the Renaissance composer Orlande de Lassus, a set of chansons in 4 and 5 parts published in London in 1570. This is the only bass part in existence*

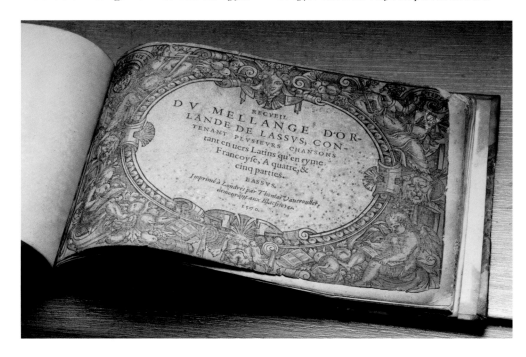

are still in pristine condition. Others, like the Tudor lute manuals, are well thumbed. The earliest work in the collection is a set of French part songs by the Flemish composer Orlande de Lassus, printed by Thomas Vautrollier, a French Huguenot refugee. This unique volume is dated 1570, the year that the Pope excommunicated Elizabeth I, and is one of the first pieces of music ever printed in this country.

As Charles II's ambassador to Louis XIV, Ralph Montagu must have attended many musical entertainments at the French court. His time there is echoed by a pair of operas by Jean-Baptiste Lully, in their first edition, and by documents relating to the French dancers and dancing masters employed by Ralph and later by his son John, who contributed enormously to the establishment of a new tradition of dance in England.

The collection also holds books of choreographic notation, following the system developed by Louis XIV's dancing master, Pierre Beauchamp, and used by the Duke's dancing master, Mr L'Abbé. The wide-ranging dance catalogue includes volumes from both court and folk traditions, and detailed eyewitness accounts of later-18th-century ballet choreographies.

Duke John was passionate about music and saw to it that his children, in particular his daughters, had every possible encouragement. He employed a succession of teachers to give them lessons, and there was a fine French harpsichord at Montagu House in London. The first edition of Handel's harpsichord suites of 1720 was most probably used to teach the Duke's daughter and heiress, Mary.

By 1720, Handel was firmly established in London, and when he started his own opera company, Duke John was one of his first subscribers. The collection has around 55 Handel operas and oratorios, many in their first edition, and several hundred arrangements for harpsichord of favourite Handel arias to be

enjoyed at home. As Master-General of the Ordnance, Duke John was responsible for commissioning from Handel one of the most famous compositions of the 18th century. George II wanted a major public celebration to mark the Treaty of Aix-la-Chapelle, which brought to an end many years of conflict in Europe. Handel delivered the *Music for the Royal Fireworks* in 1749.

In complete contrast, the collection also contains a volume of sonatas by Scarlatti, whose rise in popularity is due to this first English edition. The way these pioneering works are bound in with other keyboard items reveals the prevailing taste in home music-making at the time. Alongside them is a sonata for guitar and violin by JC Bach, some Scottish tunes in manuscript, a set of Clementi sonatas for harpsichord and flute, some songs by Thomas Arne, two waltzes and a jig, a set of songs from popular French operas, and a set of sonatas by Müthel.

A portrait by Batoni shows the 3rd Duke's

son, Lord Monthermer, holding a Corelli violin sonata and a small guitar in Italy during his extended Grand Tour in the 1750s. Many Grand Tourists went to the opera in Naples, Rome and Florence and brought back scores as souvenirs, and the collection includes three thick volumes of Italian operatic arias from the 1720s in manuscript, mostly for castrato.

But it was Monthermer's sister, Elizabeth, the Montagu heiress who inherited Boughton and married the 3rd Duke of Buccleuch, who was the family's great music enthusiast. She was given her first piano in 1770, and steadily collected music scores throughout her life. Her large keyboard section mirrors the historic transition from harpsichord to pianoforte, but her main passion was musical theatre, and her vast collection represents the genesis of the West End musical. In the wake of Handel, a whole new school of English composers was supplying nightly entertainment in London's burgeoning theatreland. Elizabeth bought the

Above left Pompeo Girolamo Batoni (1708–87)
John, Lord Brudenell, later Marquess of Monthermer (1735–70), 1758
One of Batoni's finest portraits, in which Monthermer holds a mandolin and the score of Corelli's Sixth Sonata for Violin (Op. 5)
Left *The harpsichord created for Boughton by Andrew Garlick in 2010. It is modelled on a double-manual instrument made by Goujon in Paris in 1748. The decoration is inspired by Daniel Marot's painted panels (page 131)*
Opposite, top *William Barley's well-thumbed 'The Pathway to Musicke', London, 1596*
Middle row *'Six solos for German Flute or Violin' by General John Reid (1721–1807), who founded the chair of music at Edinburgh University; John Playford's 'Brief Instructions on Playing the Cithern', London, 1666*
Bottom *Handel's suites for the harpsichord (1720) were used to teach young Mary Montagu*

piano scores of almost everything she heard, with the result that we have 85 English operas and musicals to study, and many dozens of works by the most famous continental composers of the day.

She acquired many anthologies, including the intriguing *Mrs Crokat's Favourite Melodies*, dated 1709, and Anne Armstrong's keyboard tunes, jotted down in 1752. Elizabeth's Scottish music includes more than 2,500 Highland melodies handwritten in the mid-18th century, and romantic anthologies of songs marking private Buccleuch family occasions.

The Duchess is last sighted in her regular box at the King's Theatre, Haymarket, attending the London premieres of Mozart and Rossini operas in the late 1810s. She had inadvertently created one of the great music collections, a rare window onto the musical enthusiasms of her day.

The scale and quality of the music archive were first recognised in the 1980s, but it is only in the past decade, owing to the enthusiasm of the present Duke's wife, another Elizabeth, Duchess of Buccleuch, that a crucial fresh impetus has seen the appointment of Paul Boucher as Director of the Montagu Music Collection. From this has flowed a broader research programme, involving specialists such as Jennifer Thorp, in the dance arena, and David McGuinness at the University of Glasgow, for the Scottish music.

Performance of music from the archive has helped bring life to the house through occasional concerts, and an enduring by-product has been the commissioning of a beautiful harpsichord from Andrew Garlick in 2010. The archive is once again beginning to expand; recent premieres at the house include Jonathan Dove's opera *Mansfield Park* and Julian Grant's *Sancho Dance Mix*, a suite for string orchestra after dances by Ignatius Sancho (c.1729–80), the black former slave supported in his youth by the Montagus, which was performed by the Buskaid Soweto Strings in 2014 at Boughton, and again in 2015 in Johannesburg.

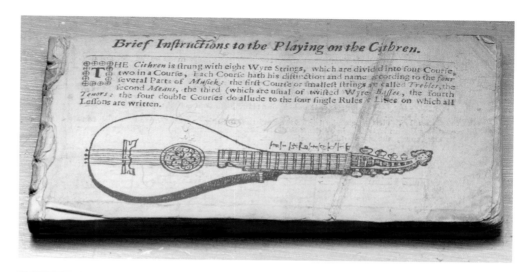

of Ralph, his son John and their families were comprehensively aided and influenced by Huguenots. The household was led by Dr Pierre Silvestre, the family physician, who doubled as inspector of building works and gardens, with M. Portal in charge of the Stables. For education, Ralph turned to Silvestre again, and a tutor, Germaine Colladon. The famous mathematician Abraham de Moivre gave his eldest son lessons in geometry, M. Camberupon improved his handwriting, Nicolas Colin taught music, and Margaret Rambour gave singing lessons.

Silvestre's annual salary of £50 appears modest considering that he also fulfilled his medical function, supplying catarrh pills and purging syrups and powders, and arranging for outside help – from M. Verdier 'for bathing and cupping some of his Grace's servants', and from M. Gerard, an oculist from Holland, to treat the Duke's eyes. French wines are much in evidence in the archives, as well as exotic foods. M. Lavigne supplied 'moist sugar for coffee' as well as cinnamon, nutmeg, vinegar, rosewater; Mme le Bonot, fresh herbs; and Anthony Gayon, anchovies and olives. M. Baptiste had a prime concession as the chocolate maker – for Christmas 1698, a bumper order of 290 pounds of chocolate is recorded.

The list of Huguenot names involved in the life of the Montagus seems never-ending – from M. Mirande the wig maker, to David Regnier the haberdasher, and from suppliers of the mundane (Jonas Durand and James Tahourdin, for household pewter) to suppliers of the exotic (M. Gouyin for a diamond necklace and rows of pearls).

A MAP of LONDON and the adjacent Country 10 Miles Round, as Survey'd and Publish'd in 16 Sheets, by John Rocque Land Surveyor, reduced into one Sheet.

CARTE DE LON

To the most High, Puissant &c. Noble Prince JOHN Duke of MONTAGUE &c. Grand Master Master of the Great Wardrobe, & Knight of the most Noble Order of the Garter

ABOVE *The Huguenot surveyor and cartographer John Rocque (c.1709–1762) made the first detailed maps of London, dedicating this 1748 edition to the Francophone 2nd Duke*
LEFT *A tea kettle made by Simon Pantin, an émigré goldsmith from Rouen, in 1715*
TOP RIGHT *A receipt signed by René and*

Thomas Pelletier in 1712 confirming that they had been paid £924 owed to them at the time of the 1st Duke's death in 1709 (page 197). The family supplied much of his giltwood furniture
RIGHT AND FAR RIGHT *The silver wine fountain with lion's masks, used to rinse wine glasses, is one of a pair supplied to Ralph in 1701*

by the Huguenot goldsmith
David Willaume (1658–1744).
The silver-gilt tea and coffee service
was made in 1712 by his former
apprentice Lewis Mettayer, his
wife's brother. The gadrooned
decoration is typically Huguenot

PREVIOUS PAGES The Little Reach and the Dead Reach, from the stone seat given by the estate to the Earl of Dalkeith on his 21st birthday in 2005 TOP ROW A beech avenue; the North Front in winter; the Duke rows his wife and a nephew in a wherry built by Mark Edwards in 2010, to a design long used by Thames boatmen and seen in Canaletto

BOTTOM ROW *The Mount blanketed in snow; the arch of the North Gate, c.1705, is mirrored by the curve of 19th-century iron gates; a view through the Stables Arch of the back drive snaking up to the Crooked Lodge; the beautiful, simple bridge that carries the main drive to the house and marks the start of the formal canal created from the humble River Ise*

The Boughton landscape

The present Duke writes of the Montagus' grand landscaping ventures and his own projects
to revive historic features and to introduce striking innovation

For 250 years the immense formal gardens at Boughton gradually, and almost entirely, disappeared from view. Six decades of creativity and enthusiasm, beginning in 1684, shortly after Ralph Montagu inherited, came grinding to a halt in 1749 with the death of his son John. Then, with house and estate passing twice in succession through the female line to families already well endowed with substantial properties of their own, benign neglect took over. Waterways silted up, woodlands were adapted for shooting, and nature and parkland enveloped the terraces and parterres. By 1796, most of the lead urns and balustrades had been removed and sold.

RIGHT *The park, with the Broad Water (left), 'Orpheus' (right) and the Mount (foreground)* BELOW *A bird's-eye view of Charles Bridgeman's plans, 1729. Visible on the right are the 1st Duke's long-lost water gardens* OPPOSITE, CLOCKWISE FROM TOP *The Grand Etang today – in 1709 the fountain reached 'above 50 feet' with the help of a windmill; the North Gate and the Lime Avenue*

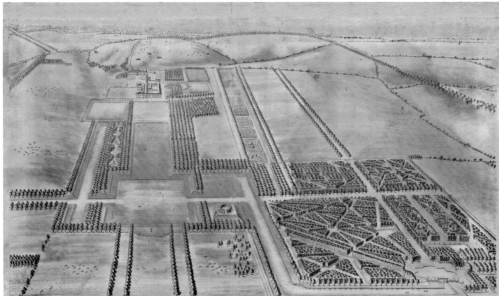

Tantalising evidence of those initial decades remained, such as a curiously symmetrical tree-covered hummock, or the majestic avenues of limes and elms before the latter tragically succumbed to disease. *Country Life* articles in 1909 talk wistfully of lost gardens, and early in the era of 'listing' – the system of planning rules to protect important heritage features – the Boughton landscape was registered as Grade I.

In 1975 all this began to change. In a move of remarkable boldness, my father had the great lake at the heart of the landscape known as the Broad Water dug out. With a new sluice gate to dam the modest River Ise, the transformation was astonishing. The Boughton West Front had a proper setting once more, with a spectacular view across water and up the avenue to the distant A43. There was an

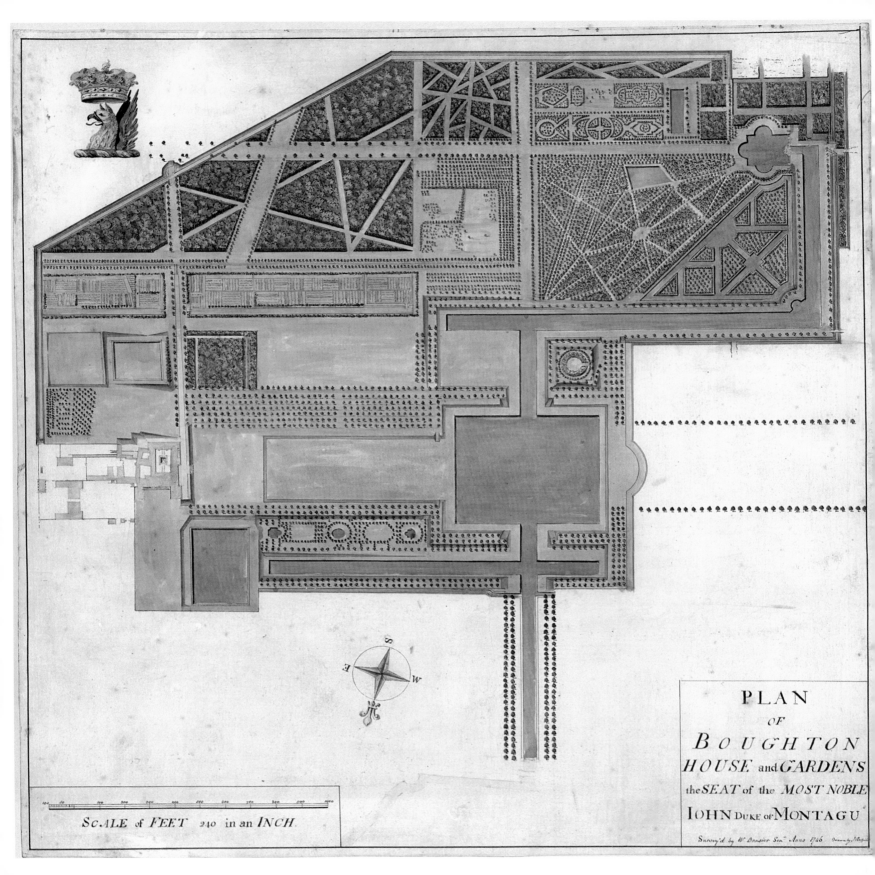

SCALE of FEET 240 in an INCH.

PLAN
OF
BOUGHTON
HOUSE and GARDENS
the SEAT of the MOST NOBLE
IOHN DUKE of MONTAGU

Survey'd by Wᵐ Bousier Senʳ Anno 1746

equally eye-catching view from the road, which, on a fine day, caused the heart to race and signalled to the family that we were almost home. Thus began the latest phase in the landscape story, a period of gradual reclamation and restoration that has now been under way for 40 years. Gradual because of the expense, most obviously, but in part too because the ruthless changes that were sometimes necessary could only be absorbed slowly.

As a family, we all rather loved the natural, unmanaged maturity of the English parkland with which we had grown up, with childhood memories of warm days, the smell of cut hay to play in, and peacefully grazing sheep in the domain of the Home Farm. But it was hard to ignore the beautifully coloured plans drawn between 1712 and 1746, or the *Vitruvius Britannicus* plan of 1722 (page 28), which showed how very different it had once been. Their help has been critical in providing a clear road map of where we could or should be heading. They illustrate the evolving taste of the times – from the fine but fussy, rigid and symmetrical parterres of the late 17th century, to the free flow into the wider countryside that one feels the 2nd Duke was grasping at, and which certainly echoed what his contemporaries were doing, advised by William Kent and others.

Known as 'John the Planter' because of his obsession with establishing avenues, the 2nd Duke appears to have been his own man in refashioning the Boughton landscape, although we know that plans by Charles Bridgeman, a pioneer of naturalistic gardening,

OPPOSITE *A plan of the gardens by William Brasier, 1746, showing them in their final state under the 2nd Duke, with his extensions to the wood garden (top left) still called The Wilderness* RIGHT *The Lily Pond, the old monastic stew pond overlooking the house, supplied it with fish from the 1st Sir Edward's day into the 20th century* TOP RIGHT *'Life Force', by Angela Conner, 2013*

were being worked to in the late 1720s. Even then the Duke was constrained by the template of canals and lakes, with their straight lines and right angles, and early avenues that his father, Ralph, had bequeathed him.

Hugely influenced by what he had seen both at Versailles and elsewhere in Europe, Ralph had appointed a Dutchman, Leonard van der Meulen, as his head gardener in 1685, and they were to work together for almost a quarter of a century. Without doubt Ralph overreached himself, as had Louis XIV, with the extent of his stone basins, statuary and fountains. A contemporary account by the Rev. John Morton recorded 'an octagon basin whose Circumference is 216 yards which in

the middle has a jet d'eau whose height is above 50 feet, surrounded with other jets d'eau', as well as a 'Cascade with Five Falls' and 'a line of jets d'eau in number Thirteen'.

It was with almost undisguised glee that Charles Hatton, a neighbour at nearby Kirby Hall, wrote in a letter in 1694: 'Here is great talk of vast gardens at Boughton but I heard my Lord Montagu is very much concerned that ye water with which he had hoped to make so fine fountains hath failed his expectations.' It is hardly surprising that many of them were removed by John, leaving sunken grass hollows still betraying where they once were, and to this day the water problem remains. The canals rapidly become choked with algae, with insufficient flow in the summer months to flush them through. The Lily Pond, on the south side of the house, is the only water body with sufficient elevation to power fountains, and the pond is fed by tiny springs, which would swiftly be drained.

Restoration of any landscape is a slow and painstaking process, even with all the technology and machinery at our disposal, which makes the achievement of hundreds of labourers with carts and horses in the late

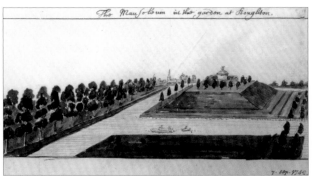

GRAND DESIGNS

TOP LEFT *The 1st Duke's cascade, drawn by the Rev. William Stukeley in 1742, flowing into the Star Pond, which was the final feature in the designed landscape, just below Weekley village*

TOP RIGHT *Stukeley's pen-and wash study of the 2nd Duke's Mount, 1742, with Weekley church in the distance. The yews were planted on the summit but his mausoleum never materialised. Both drawings are now in the Bodleian Library, Oxford*

ABOVE LEFT *An aerial view of 'Orpheus', completed in 2009, shows the Golden Section terrace with the stone rill and the sunken pool, and the 18th-century Mount beyond. The designer, Kim Wilkie, is just visible in a corner of the pool*

MAIN PICTURE *A view of the Mount, with its solitary cedar tree, home to a dozen or more nesting herons. Over the centuries the man-made hummock had become a woodland, but in 2008 the trees were removed and the sides of the hummock were resculpted to create the base of a pyramid. In 1745 the 2nd Duke had the very modern idea of holding civil wedding ceremonies on the Mount, as suggested by his friend Stukeley, who was both an Anglican clergyman and an ordained druid*

17th century all the more awesome. Boughton is particularly challenging because of its scale. The formal design covers some 100 acres, and that does not count the 450 acres of parkland beyond, embraced by the original 15th-century Deer Park, nor the 33 miles of avenues whose tentacles stretch far into the countryside. The sense of achievement that follows naturally from the number-crunching – three miles of 19th-century fencing replaced, two miles of lime avenues replanted, 70,000 cubic metres of silt dug

TOP LEFT *The steel cube, part of 'Orpheus'*
ABOVE *Grass steps, each one edged with box, lead up from the Lily Pond*
ABOVE RIGHT
The path to the Wilderness. Madame Alfred Carrière and Albertine roses cover the walls of the West Front
RIGHT *A yew arch*

The Montagu Monuments of Weekley and Warkton

The Montagus of Boughton are commemorated by a series of tombs and sculptures, some austere, others magnificent, in two nearby villages

Within living memory, family members used to make their way to Sunday church services by walking through the park to either St Mary the Virgin in Weekley or St Edmund's in Warkton. These two enchanting villages are among six embraced by the 11,500-acre Boughton Estate – the others are Geddington, Grafton Underwood, Little Oakley and Newton in the Willows. Churches in the other villages were certainly visited, and the larger St Mary Magdalene in Geddington was the venue for the wedding of the present Duke's brother Damian and his wife, Elizabeth. But the historic churches in Weekley and Warkton hold a particular significance for the family. There they find themselves among generations of Montagus and Montagu Douglas Scotts, some buried in ornate coffins below, others commemorated by simple tablets on the walls or by some of the most magnificent memorials in any village church in England.

Boughton lies within Weekley parish, and St Mary the Virgin, being the closest to the house, a 15-minute walk along an old driveway, is the resting place of the first four Montagus. In the north aisle, known as the Montagu Chapel,

ABOVE *The effigy of the 1st Sir Edward Montagu in the north aisle of the Church of St Mary the Virgin, Weekley, is carved from alabaster and would originally have been painted. Traces of red survive in the folds of his robes and on the pillow*

LEFT *The church, with the parish war memorial on the right and the Montagu Almshouse, founded as the Montagu Hospital in 1611 by the 1st Lord Montagu, on the left. The present Duke's great-uncle Lord George Scott lived here with his wife, the celebrated portrait painter Molly Bishop. It faces the park gates, which lead back to Boughton past the village cricket pitch*

is the recumbent effigy of the 1st Sir Edward, who died in 1557, his pointed features all the more severe in death, recalling his role as a Lord Chief Justice to Henry VIII. Surrounding a shield with the Montagu arms is Sir Edward's motto MILLE DOULEURS POUR UNE PLEASOIR ('For one pleasure a thousand sorrows').

Sir Edward's hands are tightly clasped in prayer, as are those of his son, the 2nd Sir Edward, who died in 1602 and lies here beside his wife, Elizabeth. But their tomb is more flamboyant, with an ornate canopy on Corinthian columns. The 2nd Sir Edward is clothed in simple armour, whereas his wife wears an elaborate ruff, complemented at her feet by the extraordinary pleats of her dress. Given that Sir Edward had left instructions that 'there be no pompe made at my funeral nor black given', one feels that his family may have compensated with this magnificent memorial.

A substantial monument with standing figures commemorates the 3rd Sir Edward, later the 1st Lord Montagu, and his first wife in her home parish at Chiddingly, East Sussex (page 12), but at Weekley he is remembered with a wall plaque and crest supported by Tuscan columns. He was interred in 1644 in the graveyard, as his will directed, next to his second 'sweet, faithful Companion', Frances Cotton, who died, aged 34, in 1620. He was the founder of the nearby Almshouse and a supporter of the tiny village school beside it.

The first wife of Ralph, 1st Duke of Montagu, another Elizabeth, was buried in St Edmund's in Warkton, and he instructed that he should be laid to rest beside her. He wanted the funeral to be 'very private', with only two coaches, and to cost 'as little as conveniently'. There is no grand memorial, nor even a simple plaque.

The deaths of his son John and his wife, Mary, in 1749 and 1751 respectively, were managed very differently, resulting in the dramatic transformation of this simple church dating back to Saxon times. The moving force was their daughter Mary, married to the Earl of

TOP *The Church of St Edmund's, Warkton. The tower bears the arms of the 1st Sir Edward*
ABOVE *The chancel was rebuilt by the Huguenot sculptor Louis-François Roubiliac in 1754 to house his memorials to the 2nd Duke and Duchess*

OPPOSITE, LEFT *The elaborate monument at Weekley built for the 2nd Sir Edward and his wife*
TOP RIGHT AND CENTRE *Elizabeth, wife of the 2nd Sir Edward, her hands raised in prayer, her small feet protruding from her much-pleated dress*
BOTTOM *The plaque to the 3rd Sir Edward, who was made 1st Lord Montagu by James I in 1621*

Cardigan. She was made the heiress to Boughton, to the chagrin of her elder sister Isabella, and there is a strong sense here of a debt being repaid. Mary took great trouble in commissioning perhaps the greatest sculptor of the age, Louis-François Roubiliac (c.1705–62), and in arranging for her father's monument, perhaps originally destined for Westminster Abbey, to be placed opposite that of his wife in this small country church.

Mary herself was the subject of an equally stunning but very different tableau by Peter Mathias van Gelder, commissioned after her death in 1775 by her daughter Elizabeth Montagu, by then Duchess of Buccleuch. The quartet of major monuments is completed by that of Elizabeth herself, who returned to her Northamptonshire roots late in life and was buried here with a rather pedestrian monument by the Scottish sculptor Thomas Campbell.

Both St Edmund's and St Mary the Virgin have wall plaques to other family descendants, but later Dukes of Buccleuch and their wives are buried and commemorated in Scotland.

Below JOHN, 2ND DUKE OF MONTAGU
It used to be said that Roubiliac's memorial for Duke John, who died in 1749, was intended for Westminster Abbey. His daughter Mary, however, was determined that both her parents be commemorated in St Edmund's, Warkton. Roubiliac portrays the grieving widow looking up plaintively at the Duke's profile in a medallion held by Charity, as a weeping child snuffs out the torch of life. She holds the Lesser George of the Order of the Garter, the high honour he received. The cannon and cannonballs on the right reflect his position as Master-General of the Ordnance

RIGHT MARY, 2ND DUCHESS OF MONTAGU
Roubiliac's memorial for Duke John's wife, Mary, who died two years later, represents the allegory of the three Fates weaving the tapestry of life. Standing in the foreground with clippers in her right hand and a skull symbolising death, Atropos has cut the thread of life, which runs from a spindle held by Clotho to another held by a small boy below. Lachesis, who determines its length and thus the span of life, raises her hand in dismay as the thread is cut short

LEFT MARY, 3RD DUCHESS OF MONTAGU
The monument by Peter Mathias van Gelder for
Mary, daughter of the 2nd Duke and Duchess,
who died in 1775, was the third to be fitted in
the chancel that she had built. Once attributed to
Robert Adam, this wonderfully fluid creation
sits above a plaque with descriptive verses by
Henry Lyte, tutor to her son, Lord Monthermer:

> *To ev'ry Wretch thy bounteous Alms*
> *Gave Raiment, Food or healing Balms.*
> *No wonder then, if o'er thy Urn*
> *Poor orphan Babes & Widows mourn*
> *Heav'n gains a holy Saint 'tis true*
> *But They have lost their Montagu*

BELOW ELIZABETH MONTAGU,
3RD DUCHESS OF BUCCLEUCH
The heiress of the last Duke of Montagu died in
1827. Walter Francis, 5th Duke of Buccleuch,
commissioned Thomas Campbell to sculpt this
memorial to his grandmother. Morpheus, the god
of dreams (on the right), has snuffed out a long
torch indicative of her great age (she died at 83)

Conservation of the Montagu Monuments

A service rededicating the Montagu Monuments in St Edmund's, Warkton, led by the Bishop of Peterborough in April 2015, celebrated the completion of a conservation project many years in the planning.

For some time the five-yearly reports on the church fabric had highlighted a number of problems, in particular the dangerous corrosion of the iron rods inside the monument to Duke John that supported the life-size figures of his wife and Charity. Various small marble elements had broken away and, without intervention, the monument might simply have fallen apart.

Further problems had been caused by efforts to keep past congregations warm by using coke-fuelled heaters. This had resulted in a soot deposit which, when combined with moisture on the cold marble, turned acidic,

ABOVE *Poultices and steam-cleaning reveal the texture of the drapery in Van Gelder's memorial to Mary, 3rd Duchess of Montagu*
RIGHT *The figures represent the distress of orphans and women championed and supported by Mary. An angel eases their grief by pointing to the place in Heaven where the Duchess has gone*

eating away at the surface as well as giving it a dirty appearance. These problems had been exacerbated by earlier conservation attempts to clean the surfaces by using Lux flakes and dousing them with water.

After several years of investigation and planning, a partnership between the Buccleuch Living Heritage Trust and the Parochial Church Council of St Edmund's Church won the all-important support of the Heritage Lottery Fund (HLF), which enabled Skillingtons, the specialist stone conservators, to begin nine months of painstaking work in the spring of 2014.

Duke John's monument had to be dismantled completely down to its rubble core, which, it became apparent, was composed of the remains of stone tracery from the church's earlier medieval chancel.

Fascinating aspects of Roubiliac's techniques were also uncovered. Poultices were applied to all four monuments to remove the polluted surface and to reveal the gleaming white marble as it had originally appeared, along with hidden details, including the way Roubiliac evoked different textures, such as silk or fur. Recent research undertaken by Prof. Phillip Lindley has cast light on the process of commissioning the monuments and how the chancel, with its unusual large, clear east window, was rebuilt.

The project to restore the monuments was managed by the Prince's Regeneration Trust and gathered broad support from many generous friends and organisations, including the Finnis Scott Foundation, the Georgian Group, the Leche Trust and the Northamptonshire Churches Trust.

As part of the HLF grant funding agreement, a number of learning initiatives are included in the programme, and the Monuments are now open for view at specified times throughout the year – details can be found on the Boughton House website (page 232).

Boughton timeline *The building's transformation from Tudor manor house to England's Versailles, and the Dukes*

The Tudor manor

The 17th century sees Ralph Montagu transform Boughton into a palatial homage to Versailles. Painted ceilings, exotic furnishings, brilliant Huguenot artistry all stun his neighbours, as do the largest formal gardens in England.

Duke John's water gardens

The 3rd Duke and Duchess – as well as their son John, on his Grand Tour – add greatly to the collection. They commission monuments from Roubiliac and buy remarkable paintings across Europe, among them a Leonardo and several Rembrandts. They choose to live elsewhere and Boughton stands still.

The 1st Sir Edward Montagu, Chief Justice to Henry VIII, buys the manor of Boughton and extends the Great Hall to create the largest Great Chamber in Northamptonshire. His son completes the West Front, creating the Fish Court. Their legacy includes tapestries and the house's remarkable rugs. Their effigies adorn the parish church of St Mary the Virgin, Weekley.

Queen Elizabeth I , 1595

Duke Ralph's North Front

The network of canals and lakes is extended and 30 miles of lime and elm avenues added by Planter John, the 2nd Duke, who creates some of the most beautiful rooms in the house.

The Buccleuch Leonardo

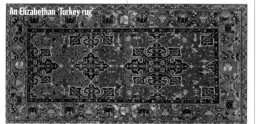
The Great Hall

The West Front in 1890

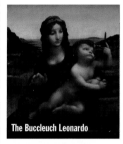

An Elizabethan 'Turkey rug'

Edward, 2nd Lord Montagu 1616–84 + Anne Winwood

Lady Mary Montagu 1715–75, daughter of John, 2nd Duke of Montagu

+ George Brudenell, Earl of Cardigan 1712–90, made 3rd Duke of Montagu

John, 2nd Duke of Montagu 1690–1749

+ Lady Mary Churchill 1689–1751

Edward, 1st Lord Montagu 1562–1644 + Elizabeth Jeffrey (above) d.1611

+ Frances Cotton d.1620

+ Ann Crouch d.1648

The 1st Sir Edward Montagu c.1490–1557

The 2nd Sir Edward Montagu 1531–1602 + Elizabeth Harington

Ralph, 1st Duke of Montagu 1638–1709 + Elizabeth Wriothesley (above) d.1690

+ Elizabeth, Duchess of Albemarle 1654–1734

The Boughton Park, 1729

Drumlanrig's Rembrandt

1500   **1550**   **1600**   **1650**   **1700**   **1750**

nd Duchesses who have left their mark by adding to its beauty

Drumlanrig Castle, Dumfriesshire

Elizabeth Montagu's love match in 1767 with the young Henry, 3rd Duke of Buccleuch, unites the Montagus with two of Scotland's great families, the Scotts and the Douglases.

Lady Elizabeth Montagu
1743–1827
+ Henry, 3rd Duke of Buccleuch, 5th Duke of Queensberry
1746–1812

Charles, 4th Duke of Buccleuch, 6th Duke of Queensberry
1772–1819
+ The Hon. Harriet Townshend
1773–1814

Bowhill House in the Scottish Borders

The 5th Duke and Duchess buy Sèvres porcelain and add to the French furniture. They rebuild Montagu House in Whitehall but refuse to rip out Boughton's Great Hall ceiling. Their son Charles Montagu Douglas Scott moves into the Dower House.

Walter Francis, 5th Duke of Buccleuch, 7th Duke of Queensberry
1806–84
+ Lady Charlotte Anne Thynne
1811–95

As Boughton sleeps, the principal Buccleuch seat remains Dalkeith, near Edinburgh. Much time is spent in the Scottish Borders.

Dalkeith Palace

Boughton comes back to life with the 6th Duke and Duchess. Plaster and panelling are renewed and new bedrooms added. The West Front is restored.

William, 6th Duke of Buccleuch, 8th Duke of Queensberry
1831–1914
+ Lady Louisa Hamilton
1836–1912

John, 7th Duke of Buccleuch, 9th Duke of Queensberry
1864–1935
+ Lady Margaret Bridgeman
1872–1954

As the 7th Duke retreats from Dalkeith Palace and Montagu House, the great country houses – Boughton, Drumlanrig and Bowhill – are filled with their glories.

The 8th Duke and Duchess lighten up the rooms, entertaining lavishly in summer.

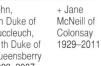

Walter, 8th Duke of Buccleuch, 10th Duke of Queensberry
1894–1973
+ Mollie Lascelles
1900–1993

The Carlin Bureau, 1749

Jennifer Thorp with Les Corps Eloquents, 2014

The Garlick Harpsichord, 2010

John, 9th Duke of Buccleuch, 11th Duke of Queensberry
1923–2007
+ Jane McNeill of Colonsay
1929–2011

The present Duke's parents bring a fresh, knowledgeable eye to conservation. They restore the Broad Water, bring back the pool and fountain to the Fish Court and create its white garden. The house is opened to the public and the Living Landscape Trust educational charity is set up. The Stables are saved from collapse.

Richard, 10th Duke of Buccleuch, 12th Duke of Queensberry
b.1954
+ Lady Elizabeth Kerr b.1954

2014 Walter, Earl of Dalkeith, marries Elizabeth Cobbe

Orpheus, 2011

The present Duke and Duchess set out to renew the landscape and commission the landmark *Orpheus*. A new harpsichord is made for Boughton and the spirit of 18th-century music is revived.

The Grand Etang, 2014

1800   1850   1900   1950   2000

Chronology of key events

1292 Edward I erects the Eleanor Cross in Geddington as a memorial to his Queen, Eleanor of Castile. The royal hunting ground of Rockingham Forest covers swathes of countryside.

1348–50 The Black Death kills an estimated 1.5 million in England. The village of Bucca's 'tun' that lay northeast of the Stables declines.

c.1370 First evidence of the Montagu family, sometimes called Ladde, settling in Northamptonshire and living at Hanging Houghton, 14 miles to the west.

1448 Richard Ladde adpots his mother's maiden name, Montagu.

1473 The park at Boughton is enclosed by the then owner, Richard Whetehills.

1509 Henry VII, who established the Tudor dynasty when he defeated Richard III at Bosworth Field, 30 miles to the north of Boughton, dies and is succeeded by Henry VIII.

1528 Edward Montagu buys part of Boughton from a Calais merchant and completes the purchase in 1536. Around this time the Great Hall is built and the house extended.

1537 He achieves his highest office as Lord Chief Justice of the Common Pleas and is knighted.

1547 He acts as an Executor when Henry VIII dies.

1587 The 2nd Sir Edward Montagu witnesses the Execution of Mary Queen of Scots in nearby Fotheringhay Castle. The next year, he helps raise troops against the Spanish Armada.

1603 James VI of Scotland becomes James I of England, uniting the crowns and launching the Stuart dynasty.

1604 The King attends a feast in the Great Hall at Boughton and is served by all six of the 2nd Sir Edward's sons.

1605 The 3rd Sir Edward escapes implication in the Gunpowder Plot and proposes Guy Fawkes Day as an official day of celebration.

1611 The Montagu Hospital, now the Almshouse in Weekley, is built.

1621 The 3rd Sir Edward is made the 1st Lord Montagu by James I.

1644 He dies under house arrest by Parliament. His son escorts Charles I into captivity at nearby Holdenby.

1649 After the execution of Charles I, the 2nd Lord Montagu retires from public life in dismay.

1660 His elder son, Ned, helps escort Charles II to London at the Restoration.

1665 Ned is killed in the sea battle of Bergen, a year after his fall from favour at court when he squeezed the hand of the Queen, Catherine of Braganza.

1669 Ralph Montagu is sent for the first time to Louis XIV's court in France as the envoy of Charles II.

1675 He builds the first Montagu House in Bloomsbury.

1678 With his involvement in the Exclusion Crisis and the fall of Danby, he falls out of favour.

1684 Ralph inherits Boughton and engages the gardener Leonard van der Meulen to create the vast landscape. Montagu House is rebuilt after a fire.

1689 Ralph supports William and Mary in the Glorious Revolution and becomes Earl of Montagu.

c.1690 Construction of Boughton's Versailles-style North Front begins.

1695 William III visits Boughton.

1705 The North Front is completed with the building of the Stables.

1705 Ralph is made 1st Duke of Montagu by Queen Anne. His heir, John, marries Lady Mary Churchill, daughter of the Duke of Marlborough.

1709 John succeeds his father as 2nd Duke of Montagu.

c.1715 Duke John begins to remodel and extend the Tudor West Front.

1718 He is appointed a Knight of the Garter by George I and becomes a director of the newly founded Royal Academy of Music.

1720 He establishes the 'New French Theatre' in the Haymarket.

1722 Duke John launches his abortive expedition to take St Vincent and St Lucia in the Caribbean.

c.1730 He has the new Montagu House constructed overlooking the Thames in Whitehall.

1740 He becomes Master-General of the Ordnance.

1742 The Rev. William Stukeley draws plans for a mausoleum on the Mount in the park at Boughton.

1745 John buys the Chinese Pavilion.

1749 He plays a pivotal role in the first performance of Handel's *Music for the Royal Fireworks*, celebrating the end of the War of the Austrian Succession. On his death his daughter Mary and her husband, George, Earl of Cardigan, inherit the bulk of the estate.

1751 The Cardigans' son, Lord Monthermer, heads off for a decade of travel in France and Italy.

1759 Montagu House, Bloomsbury, becomes the new British Museum.

1755 Roubiliac's monuments to the 2nd Duke and Duchess are completed in St Edmund's, Warkton.

1756 The Cardigans acquire Leonardo's *Madonna of the Yarnwinder* and the Colbert Cabinet at the Tallard sale in Paris.

1756 The dukedom of Montagu is revived for the Cardigans.

1767 Elizabeth Montagu marries Henry, 3rd Duke of Buccleuch, and becomes heir to Boughton on the death of her brother John in 1770.

1782 The letters of Ignatius Sancho, the former slave supported by the family, are published.

1790 George, 3rd Duke of Montagu, dies and Boughton passes to Elizabeth but lapses gently into disuse.

1812 Henry, 3rd Duke of Buccleuch, inherits the Douglas dukedom of Queensberry and the seat of Drumlanrig Castle in Scotland.

1827 Elizabeth dies. Her memorial by Thomas Campbell is erected beside the family tombs in Warkton.

1831–32 Walter Francis, 5th Duke of Buccleuch, and his wife, Charlotte Anne, buy the Sèvres porcelain. They subsequently expand the collections.

1857 Kettering Station opens; the 5th Duke makes it a condition that a line crossing his land must be diverted to benefit Kettering.

1862 The new Montagu House in Whitehall is built by William Burn.

1865 Admiral Lord Charles Scott, 4th son of the 5th Duke, moves into the Dower House. He and his son, Sir David Scott, who dies in 1986, will occupy it for a total of 120 years.

1909 A *Country Life* article talks wistfully of Boughton's lost gardens.

1911 Modern plumbing is introduced and the Great Hall is panelled.

1916 The State Bed is given to the Victoria and Albert Museum.

c.1920 Treasures from Dalkeith House and Montagu House are shared among Boughton, Bowhill and Drumlanrig.

1939–45 During the Second World War the house is used for safekeeping by the British Museum, the Science Museum and Westminster Abbey. The park becomes a military transit camp, then a POW camp. An airfield behind the house is used by US bombers.

1950s Walter, 8th Duke, and his wife, Mollie, engage John Fowler to help redecorate the Drawing Room and lighten up the interiors.

1967 Dutch elm disease destroys the elm avenues.

1975 The 8th Duke restores the Broad Water, and the Stables are saved from subsidence and collapse.

1992 *Boughton House: The English Versailles*, the first major study of the house, is published.

2005 The Boughton State Bed returns to the State Rooms, on loan from the Victoria and Albert Museum.

Further reading on Boughton

2008 Kim Wilkie embarks on *Orpheus*, an important addition to the landscape.
2010 A harpsichord is commissioned from Andrew Garlick.
2012 The premiere of Jonathan Dove's opera *Mansfield Park* in the Great Hall.
2014 The Grand Etang and its fountain are another milestone in the restoration of the park.
2015 The exhibition *The Huguenots at Boughton* marks the 3rd centenary of Louis XIV's death.
2016 Boughton celebrates Handel's legacy in the Montagu music archives.

A NOTE ON NAMES

Three of the cast in the story of Boughton have complex title trajectories. When referring to them, we generally use their final names and titles. Ralph Montagu is commonly referred to as 1st Duke of Montagu, although when he was Ambassador to France he was plain Mr Montagu, and on his father's death in 1684, he became the 3rd Lord Montagu. William and Mary elevated him to Earl of Montagu in 1689. He only became Duke of Montagu in 1705, four years before his death.

Mary Montagu, heiress of the 2nd Duke, married George, Lord Brudenell, in 1730, briefly becoming Lady Brudenell. On the death of his father two years later, they rose to be Earl and Countess of Cardigan. For most of their lives, they were known as the Cardigans. In 1766 the dukedom of Montagu, which could not pass via the female line, was recreated for them. Thus, although technically the 1st Duke of the 2nd creation, George is thought of as being the 3rd Duke.

Their son, John, would have been known to his contemporaries as Lord Brudenell, but benefited for the last four years of his life from his parents' elevation, becoming Marquess of Monthermer.

BOOKS

BOUGHTON AND ITS COLLECTIONS
The most comprehensive overview is *Boughton House: The English Versailles*, edited by **Tessa Murdoch** (Faber & Faber with Christie's, 1992). **John Heward and Robert Taylor**, *Country Houses of Northamptonshire* (Royal Commission on Historical Monuments, 1996). The chapter on Boughton is the best architectural study.

THE MONTAGUS OF BOUGHTON
Steven Hicks, *Ralph, 1st Duke of Montagu (1638–1709)* (New Generation, 2015). *Estate letters from the time of John, 2nd Duke of Montagu 1709–1739*, transcribed by **Alan Toseland**, ed. PH McKay and DN Hall (Northants Record Soc., 2013). **Joan Wake**, *The Brudenells of Deene* (Cassell, 1953). **Esther S. Cope**, *The Life of a Public Man: Edward, 1st Baron Montagu of Boughton, 1562–1644* (American Philosophical Society, 1981).

FRENCH INFLUENCES
Helen Jacobsen, *Luxury and Power: The Material World of the Stuart Diplomat, 1660–1714* (OUP, 2011). **Paul Boucher and Tessa Murdoch**, 'Montagu House, Bloomsbury: a French household in London, 1673–1733', in *A History of the French in London*, ed. **Debra Kelly and Martin Cornyck** (Inst. of Hist. Research, 2013).

CONTENTS OF THE HOUSE
Tessa Murdoch ed., *Noble Households: Eighteenth Century Inventories of Great English Houses: A Tribute to John Cornforth* (John Adamson, 2006). **Francis Russell**, 'The Hanging and Display of Pictures, 1700–1850' in *The Fashioning and Functioning of the English House*, ed. Gervase Jackson-Stops (Nat. Gallery of Art, Washington, 1989).

MAGAZINES AND JOURNALS

ARCHITECTURE
John Cornforth's series in *Country Life*, 'Boughton House, Northamptonshire' (Sept. 3, 10 and 17, 1970, and Feb. 28, March 4 and 11, 1971), lays the foundation for all later scholarly study.

Gervase Jackson-Stops, 'Daniel Marot and the 1st Duke of Montagu', *Dutch Art History Yearbook* (1980). Older articles in *Country Life*: **Avery Tipping** (Jan. 30, Feb. 6, 1909) and **Margaret Jourdain** (Nov. 26, Dec. 3, 1932).

ARMOURY
Paul Wilcock, 'The Armoury of His Grace the Duke of Buccleuch and Queensbury', *Arms and Armour* (vol. 9, no. 2, 2011).

CARPETS
Ian Bennett and Michael Franses, 'The Buccleuch European Carpets and Others in the Oriental Style', *HALI* (1992).

CARTOONS
Tom Campbell, 'Pope Leo X's consistorial *letto de paramento* and the Boughton House cartoons', *The Burlington Magazine* (July 1996).

FURNITURE
Geoffrey Beard and Annabel Westman, 'A French Upholsterer in England: Francis Lapiere, 1653–1714', *The Burlington Magazine* (Aug. 1993). **Adam Bowett**, 'A Group of Metal Marquetry Tables attributed to Gerrit Jensen'; **Nicola Gentle**, 'An Astonishing Survival: the Bed in the Red Room at Cotehele, Cornwall'; **Adriana Turpin**, 'The Career of Cornelius Gole: An Unrecognized Cabinetmaker' – all in *Furniture History* (vol. L, 2014). **Calin Demetrescu**, '*Le cabinet Boulle du duc de Buccleuch: une énigme résolue*'; **Mia Jackson**, '*Boulle auteur, editeur et revendeur d'estampes*' – both in *Dossier de l'Art* (Dec. 2014). **John Hardy and Adriana Turpin**, 'Cornelius Gole's Book of Ornaments: a political pattern-book', *Apollo* (197, 1993). **Tessa Murdoch**, 'Jean, René and Thomas Pelletier, a Huguenot Family of Carvers and Gilders in England 1682–1726', *The Burlington Magazine* (Nov. 1997 and June 1998); 'The king's cabinet-maker: the giltwood furniture of James Moore the Elder', *The Burlington Magazine* (June 2003).

MURALS
François Marandet, '*Boughton House: nouvelles réflexions sur la genèse et la signification du décor peint de*

"*Mister Charron*"', *Journal of British Art* (forthcoming); 'Louis Chéron (Paris, 1660 – London, 1725): four rediscovered print designs for Racine's Plays', *Prints Quarterly* (June 2015); 'A rediscovered modello for Louis Chéron's Pool at Bethesda', *The Burlington Magazine* (March 2014).

PATRONAGE
John Fleming, 'Lord Brudenell and his Bear Leader', *English Miscellany* (9, 1958). **John Cornforth**, 'Castles for a Georgian Duke', *Country Life* (Oct. 8, 1992). **Tessa Murdoch**, 'The Dukes of Montagu as patrons of the Huguenots', *Proceedings of the Huguenot Society* (XXV, 1992).

THE MONTAGU MONUMENTS
Phillip Lindley, 'Peter Mathias van Gelder's Monument to Mary, 3rd Duchess of Montagu, in St Edmund's Warkton', *The Burlington Magazine* (2013); 'Roubiliac's Monuments for the Second Duke and Duchess of Montagu and the Building of the New Chancel at Warkton in Northamptonshire', *The Walpole Society* (LXXVI, 2014). **Tessa Murdoch**, 'Spinning the thread of Life: The Three Fates, Time and Eternity', in *Burning Bright, Essays in Honour of David Bindman* (UCL, 2015); 'Roubiliac as an Architect? The bill for the Warkton monuments', *The Burlington Magazine* (Jan 1980).

ACKNOWLEDGEMENTS
Special thanks for contributing to this book in many different ways go to Lisa Brack, Michael Crick, Dr Honor Gay, Sandra Howat and Charles Lister; to Andrew Byfield for identifying flowers in the Monnoyer paintings; and to Orhan Gündüz, Niyazi Karıksız, Tamol Küçükerol and their colleagues at the printers Ofset Yapımevi. The emerging history of Boughton owes much to the archival research undertaken by Bruce Bailey, Helen Bates, Judith Hodgkinson, Prof. Phillip Lindley, Tamar Moore, Emma Purcell, Jana Schuster, Alan Toseland and the staff at the Northamptonshire Archives Service.

BOUGHTON, MAY 1955
*A day in the life of 'R', the present
Duke Richard, aged 15 months.
Members of the family seen here
in the Fish Court include
grandparents, parents, aunts, one
of his uncles and first cousins*

BOUGHTON HOUSE
Kettering
Northamptonshire
NN14 1BJ
TEL 01536 515731
info@boughtonhouse.co.uk
www.boughtonhouse.co.uk

2016 © Buccleuch
Living Heritage Trust
PUBLISHED BY
Caique Publishing Ltd
PO Box 13311,
Hawick TD9 7YF, Scotland
ISBN 978-0-9565948-5-3

DESIGN Clive Crook
COLOUR EDITOR Berrin Scott
CO-EDITORS Susana Raby,
Tony Barrell, Rose Shepherd
and Hilary Stafford-Clark
ARCHIVIST AND HISTORICAL
ADVISER Crispin Powell
MONTAGU MUSIC COLLECTION
Paul Boucher
COLLECTIONS ADVISER
Gareth Fitzpatrick
HISTORICAL LANDSCAPE
ADVISER Lance Goffort-Hall
PRINTED BY Ofset Yapımevi,
Istanbul, www.ofset.com

CREDITS
All photographs by
Fritz von der Schulenburg
unless otherwise stated.
Cover: Tom Arbor
Family albums: John McKenzie.
Works of art: Richard Shellabear,
Todd-White Art Photography.
Little Hall fireplace p7; Puckle
gun 26; Second State Room 62
by John Edwards
Aerial views: p47 by Michael
Crick, pp210, 214 by Kim Wilkie.
The park pp208, 209, 215 Gareth
Fitzpatrick, Lance Goffort-Hall.

Kim Wilkie p219 by Tessa
Traeger/National Portrait Gallery.
Chiddingly memorial p12; details
pp91, 99, 200 by Clive Crook.
Montagu Monuments by Tom
Arbor; p226 by Paul Boucher.
Carpets pp13, 14, murals pp55,
67; silver p205 by Mark Asher
Portrait p195, Norman Parkinson
Ltd/Norman Parkinson Archive
William Stukeley drawings p214,
The Bodleian Library, Oxford.
The Great Hall p39 *Country Life*.
Sèvres porcelain: pp168–169 by
Mark Usher Photography.